Getting Your
First Job

Books to change your life and work.
Accessible, easy to read and easy to act on –
other titles in the **How To** series include:

Writing a CV that Works
How to develop and use your key marketing tool

Enhancing Your Employability
How to make sure you achieve a fulfilling and rewarding career

Applying for a Job
How to sell your skills and experience to a prospective employer

Passing That Interview
Your step-by-step guide to achieving success

Staying Ahead at Work
How to develop a winning portfolio of work skills and attitudes

The **How To series** now contains
around 200 titles in the following categories:

Business & Management
Computer Basics
General Reference
Jobs & Careers
Living & Working Abroad
Personal Finance
Self-Development
Small Business
Student Handbooks
Successful Writing

Send for a free copy of the latest catalogue to:
How To Books
Customers Services Dept.
Plymbridge House, Estover Road
Plymouth PL6 7PZ, Unkited Kingdom
Tel: 01752 202301   Fax: 01752 202331
http://www.howtobooks.co.uk

Getting Your
First Job

*How to get the job that will
give you the right start*

PENNY HITCHIN
2nd edition

How To Books

First published by How To Books Ltd, 3 Newtec Place,
Magdalen Road, Oxford OX4 1RE, United Kingdom.
Tel: (01865) 793806. Fax: (01865) 248780.
email: info@howtobooks.co.uk
http://www.howtobooks.co.uk

British Library Cataloguing in Publication Data.
A catalogue record for this book is available from
the British Library.

Second edition 1999

Cartoons by Mike Flanagan
Cover design by Shireen Nathoo Design
Cover image by PhotoDisc

Produced for How To Books by Deer Park Productions
Typeset by Kestrel Data, Exeter
Printed and bound by Cromwell Press Ltd, Trowbridge, Wiltshire

NOTE: The material contained in this book is set out in good
faith for general guidance and no liability can be accepted
for loss or expense incurred as a result of relying in particular
circumstances on statements made in the book. Laws and
regulations are complex and liable to change, and readers should
check the current position with the relevant authorities before
making personal arrangements.

Contents

List of Illustrations

Preface

What does this book offer you?
- Ideas
- Information
- Support
- Encouragement

Looking for a job can be a demoralising experience. Unless you strike it lucky at an early stage, it's hard to maintain the necessary self-confidence and enthusiasm. *Getting Your First Job* is designed to help you take a constructive and positive approach to the business of starting your career. It:

- Gives pragmatic information about the fast-changing and volatile job market and an insight into the strange mind-set of that mythical, omnipotent creature 'the employer'.

- Contains self-assessment material and quizzes to help you identify your strengths, skills and potential. It is designed to be fun as well as being a practical, confidence-boosting resource.

- Sets out to help you uncover the skills and talents which make you employable and suggests strategies for presenting those in the most positive way.

- Provides upbeat strategies to boost morale and maintain motivation.

As we enter the twenty-first century *Getting Your First Job* has been revised and up-dated, to incorporate information about changes in the job market, developments in information and communications technology and employment projections.

Armed with this inside information, I hope you will succeed in getting one foot in the door and the other on the ladder. I hope you find the book useful and enjoyable. Happy job hunting!

Penny Hitchin

1

Why Work?

I like work: it fascinates me. I can sit and look at it for hours.
Jerome K. Jerome

If work were a good thing, the rich would have found a way of keeping it to themselves.
Haitian proverb

Work is only for people who don't know how to fish.
Scottish saying

WHAT DOES WORK OFFER?

What are you looking for from your job? There is one obvious answer – money – but there's more to work than pay.

People look to their work to provide them with a variety of benefits. Opportunities for meeting people, working as part of a team, learning new skills, doing something worthwhile, helping others, gaining status in the community are some of the rewards that people say their work provides. The term used to describe the non-financial benefits of work is *job satisfaction*.

WHAT DO YOU WANT FROM A JOB?

Some jobs – for example, the services – provide a whole way of life; while others give employees more opportunity to develop their life outside the workplace. Whatever you opt for, if you're going to spend 2,000 hours a year at work, let's hope you get more out of it than money.

Here are some of the things people look for:

From the tasks
People want:
• varied and meaningful work

- freedom to choose their own pace and working conditions to avoid unnecessary stress

- work that matches their abilities and interests.

From the rewards
People want:
- adequate pay

- promotion prospects

- job security

- status in the community

- jobs that are intrinsically worthwhile.

From the working environment
People want:
- to have sociable contact with other people

- to work as a member of a team

- to be treated with respect and in a constructive way

- to work in decentralised structures

- to work without elaborate hierarchies

- to have clear job roles without conflict of confusion.

How about you, are there other things you would add?

REASONS FOR WORKING

Here are 25 reasons why people work. Can you add any others?
1. To get money.
2. To help others.
3. To get on in the world.
4. To develop myself.
5. To gain independence.

6. To contribute to the community.
7. To do something worthwhile.
8. To contribute to the economy.
9. To get perks.
10. To learn new skills.
11. To get experience.
12. To save the planet.
13. To have power.
14. To have responsibility.
15. To get out of the house.
16. To move to a new area.
17. To meet people.
18. To be respected.
19. To earn a pension.
20. To have opportunities for travel.
21. To tackle challenges.
22. To avoid the inner void.
23. To be part of an organisation.
24. To bring structure into life.
25. To keep fit.

HOW MOTIVATED ARE YOU?

This light-hearted force field exercise provides an indication of how motivated you are in your desire to work. You might find it interesting to ask some of your friends or family to complete their own force fields so that you can compare your results with them.

To complete the exercise, use the list of 25 reasons for working (above). Add any other reasons that are important to you, then pick out the 10 that are most important to you. Fill them in on the *Reasons I want to work* form on page 14.

Decide on a rating for each of your 10 reasons and write it on the form.

Use a rating system from 5 to 1 where:
   5 is very important
   4 is fairly important
   3 is a significant consideration
   2 is slightly significant
   1 is not at all important

Table 1
Reasons I want to work

Rating

1. . . . . –
2. . . . . –
3. . . . . –
4. . . . . –
5. . . . . –
6. . . . . –
7. . . . . –
8. . . . . –
9. . . . . –
10. . . . . –

Table 1 Total

Table 2
Reasons I don't want to work

Rating

1. . . . . –
2. . . . . –
3. . . . . –
4. . . . . –
5. . . . . –
6. . . . . –
7. . . . . –
8. . . . . –
9. . . . . –
10. . . . . –

Table 2 Total

Then write down 10 reasons for not working and rate them 5 to 1 according to their importance to you (use the scale as above). Write down the score for each one on the form.

Table 1	Total score for working	_____
Table 2	Total score against working	_____
Subtract 2 from 1 to give *Motivation to work* total		_____

Final score

40 or above	Whoops! Check your maths, or re-do the questionnaire paying more attention to the instructions!
30–39	You have a very strong motivation to work. Good luck in your job search.
20–29	You are fairly well motivated, but aware of the down-side of working.
10–19	You need to be more positive about work, or you'll never get a job.
0–10	Let's hope you win the lottery, or marry a millionaire because with your motivation (or lack of it) you're not going to get a job.
less than 0	You're not interested in working. Why are you bothering with this book? Sorry to trouble you!

The lifestyle wish-list

'MILLIONS WILL NOT CHANGE MY LIFE' VOWS MR MONEYBAGS

37-year-old Mark Mason collected his bumper £2.7 million jackpot cheque, paused for the photo-call, then dashed off to his regular night shift.

'I'm going to buy a new car, pay off the mortgage and have a holiday, but I plan to keep my job . . . that's where my mates are.'

Could it be you? What would you do if you won the lottery jackpot? Think about the lifestyle that you would adopt. Once you've bought everything you want, what are you going to do with your new found wealth and leisure? The fairy-tale ending of living happily ever after is just that: a fantasy. Most people have a wish-list of things they would like to buy – usually including houses, cars and holidays – but after that they actually need activities to get involved in. These may be work or hobbies, but everyone needs to stretch themselves. Life is for living, for doing things, for experiencing: for a lot of people work is an essential part of this.

WHAT CAN YOU OFFER AN EMPLOYER?

Hopefully you have qualities that employers want. But what are the qualities that employers value? That's one of those elusive 'How long is a piece of string?' questions. The answer depends on the employer and the company. Different employers look for different things: one manager may welcome a trainee's ability to 'pick up the ball and run with it' (a currently trendy management term describing the ability to take the initiative), while another might condemn exactly the same behaviour for being presumptuous and ignoring company procedures.

There's an old joke which involves conjugating expressions of firmness thus . . . 'I am firm, you are stubborn, he is a stupid old fool.' In other words, the qualities we find admirable in ourselves can be a downright nuisance when encountered in others.

Many qualities are a double-edged sword: they can be both desirable and undesirable depending entirely on the situation. One of the skills the jobseeker can usefully acquire is the ability to present themselves in the most positive light possible!

Thus, a gossiping, opinionated, techno-nerd would be better described as a sociable, computer literate and self-confident individual.

If you are modest, straight-talking and lacking in guile, you may find this a daunting prospect, but thinking positively is a vital life skill, and it is particularly important to believe in yourself and be positive about your skills, personality, ambitions and achievements.

Selling yourself

Think of a couple of different jobs which interest you. Then imagine you are in the position of the employer and are looking to recruit people for those two posts.

Use the list of characteristics below and pick out 10 which you think would be particularly important for each of the two jobs. Then give yourself a rating for each quality where:

5 describes you very well
4 describes you quite well
3 describes you some of the time
2 describes you occasionally
1 describes you hardly ever

Be realistic but positive and don't undersell yourself!

Adaptable	☐ ☐	Numerate	☐ ☐
Ambitious	☐ ☐	Objective	☐ ☐
Analytical	☐ ☐	Open-minded	☐ ☐
Articulate	☐ ☐	Optimistic	☐ ☐
Assured	☐ ☐	Persistent	☐ ☐
Concise	☐ ☐	Persuasive	☐ ☐
Creative	☐ ☐	Punctual	☐ ☐
Curious	☐ ☐	Reliable	☐ ☐
Decisive	☐ ☐	Resilient	☐ ☐
Easygoing	☐ ☐	Self-confident	☐ ☐
Enthusiastic	☐ ☐	Self-reliant	☐ ☐
Fit	☐ ☐	Sensitive	☐ ☐
Friendly	☐ ☐	Smart	☐ ☐
Good looking	☐ ☐	Sympathetic	☐ ☐
Good sense of humour	☐ ☐	Tidy	☐ ☐
Honest	☐ ☐	Tolerant	☐ ☐
Modest	☐ ☐	Trustworthy	☐ ☐
Motivated	☐ ☐	Well qualified	☐ ☐

How well do you measure up? Not too badly, is the likely answer. In that case one of your next challenges is to think of ways to convey this to someone who is in a postion to offer you a job. More on this in Chapter 4, How Do You Measure Up?

2

The Future of Work

The twenty-first century will see lots of changes in the way we live and work. In line with this the workforce profile is evolving:

- The total working population of the country is increasing.

- Women make up nearly 50% of the workforce.

- The proportion of workers under 35 is declining.

- The number of older workers is increasing.

- More part-time, temporary and contract jobs are available.

- People will routinely change careers mid-stream.

For new jobseekers in the twenty-first century, finding a full-time permanent job for life may not be an option. However, this is not a personal failure, it's something that is happening throughout our society. Job security is being replaced with job mobility as career patterns change to incorporate spells of training, part-time work and other switches of direction. The future lies in being an adaptable, enthusiastic individual, who can respond positively to challenges and opportunities.

HOW JOBS ARE CHANGING

However you look at it, work is one of the central activities of life. It has to be done to provide food, shelter, clothes, security and the care, protection and education of children.

Our ancestors made no distinction between work and leisure. Everything they did was geared towards continuing their existence. However, as society developed, it became possible to regard work as a separate activity, possibly done by some people for the benefit of others.

Towards the end of the eighteenth century the invention of the mechanical steam engine heralded the Industrial Revolution which set a new pattern of work for most people. For nearly two centuries, the wealth and prosperity of the country depended on manufacturing. Industry was labour intensive and employed lots of strong operatives and craftsmen.

In the last decades advances in information technology have transformed working practices in commerce and industry. Sophisticated machines have become part of everyday working life. Automation has taken over many repetitive and routine tasks, and caused radical change to jobs in shops, offices, factories and warehouses across the land.

In 'post-industrial' societies like Britain, the pattern of work is changing fundamentally in ways that will affect every one of us. As the technology continues to develop, the jobs that are available and the skills that are needed are constantly evolving.

We are living in times of great change. As technology races ahead, concern about the environment is mounting. Full employment – the situation where there are enough jobs so that everyone who wants to work can find employment – may be a thing of the past.

Society faces the challenge of finding ways of generating wealth that don't harm the planet, and that provide satisfying and fulfilling employment for people.

OUT   job security
IN   short-term contracts or self-employment

OUT   jobs for unskilled labourers and operatives
IN   opportunities for adaptable people with 'transferable skills'

OUT   jobs in manufacturing
IN   jobs in service industries

OUT   rigid demarcation between different jobs
IN   multi-skilled workers who can turn their hand to different roles

OUT   the notion of a job for life
IN   a mix of short-term contracts; changes in direction; spells of unemployment; part-time work; training and education

OUT	companies' in-house departments running non-core functions
IN	outsourcing – sub-contracting specialist functions out to consultants

HOW THE JOB MARKET IS CHANGING

Predicting what is going to happen in the labour market is a complicated and speculative business which inevitably relies on guesswork. Factors affecting employment include the number of people in the working population, the state of the economy (both at home and overseas) and developments in technology.

Labour Market Skills Trends 1998/9, a report published by the Department for Education and Employment identified the following changes in the job market between 1981 and 1997:

- Total employment rose by 2.1 million.

- Financial and service sector jobs increased.

- 2.1 million new jobs for managers, professionals and technicians came into existence.

- Nearly a million manual jobs were lost.

- Part-time jobs increased by 1 million.

- 0.5 million more people became self-employed.

Projections to the year 2007 include:

- Total employment will continue to rise.

- Over 4 million people will be self-employed.

- The numbers employed in manufacturing will continue to drop.

- The numbers employed in the service sector will increase.

- Women will increase their share of jobs in most service occupations.

- A disproportionate number of new jobs will be part-time with low pay and status.

- More professional and managerial jobs will be part-time.

WHERE WILL THE GROWTH INDUSTRIES BE?

Gaze into the crystal ball and see if you come up with the right answer. Incidentally, growth in the industry doesn't necessarily mean more jobs. Growth is measured by output, productivity and profit, not by jobs created. On with the guesswork. Some trends for job-creating growth could be:

Finance

Banks, building societies, insurance companies and a host of other services are changing the way customers contact them. Instead of face-to-face meetings in local high street branches, customers pick up the phone to ring gigantic centralised telephone call centres. Operating day and night, call centre staff rely on keyboard, computer and telephone to serve customers.

Distribution

In lean, mean times no business wants its capital tied up in keeping big stocks. Fast and efficient distribution networks allow firms to operate at maximum efficiency. Over the last few years courier and delivery services have been expanding and creating new jobs.

Hotels and catering

Leisure and tourism is growing. Hotels, restaurants, bars, cafés and fast food outlets are part of a labour-intensive service industry offering lots of openings for people with and without qualifications. On the down side, the rates of pay have traditionally been low, hours are anti-social and there are lots of temporary, seasonal vacancies. However, opportunities and training abound for keen and enthusiastic staff.

Health

The combination of an ageing population profile and an increase in people's expectations (due to advances in medical research) means that the health industry will grow, providing high-tech, highly skilled medical jobs, as well as labour-intensive care work.

Education

Education and training are seen as the key to economic prosperity. With record numbers going into higher education, this sector is expanding. However, productivity gains come from cutting staff:student ratios and using techniques that cut down on staff, e.g. greater use of computers, video and other teaching tools.

Leisure

Growth areas include theme parks, entertainment centres, clubs, sports centres, laser games and arcades, virtual reality, multiplex cinemas, betting shops and casinos. The leisure industry offers lots of seasonal and part-time openings and traditionally has provided opportunities for people without qualifications. On the down side, the hours are anti-social and the rates of pay are often low. However, there are lots of opportunities for keen and enthusiastic staff to work their way up.

Environment

People are showing increased awareness of the fragile balance of the environment. Concern about changes to the climate, pollution, disposal of toxic waste and by-products is growing. This is affecting consumers' purchasing decisions. The 'polluter pays' principle and spread of environmental auditing may lead to more demand for knowledge, skills and expertise in environmental management.

Biotechnology

Biotechnology has been identified as an important technology cluster which is poised to affect industry, jobs and society. What is biotechnology? It's the name given to the application of biological organism systems or processes to manufacturing and service industries. And actually it's not new. Brewing, wine-making, leavening bread are all age-old applications of biotechnology.

Agriculture, chemicals, food and drink, waste treatment and process plants are all influenced by developments in biotechnology. Undoubtedly this will affect jobs, but whether it is going to lead to new jobs is open to speculation. Recently consumer concern about GMOS (genetically modified organisms) has forced both the government and companies to reconsider developments.

WHO WILL BE LOOKING FOR WORK?

The study of the population reveals that the population of Great Britain is ageing! Between 1988 and 1994 the number of young people who left school or college to enter the workforce fell by 30 per cent. Changes in the population mean that this reduction in numbers of young people entering the job market will become a permanent feature of the workforce. This has been called the 'demographic time-bomb' (demography is the statistical study of human populations).

In the five years between 1997 and the year 2002 the number of 25–34 year olds in the labour force will drop by a million to 6.5 million. However, there will be a million more 35–44 year olds and half a million more 45–59 year olds.

By 2002, there will be 4.5 million 16–24 year olds in the labour force, which is broadly comparable to the number in 1997. Although the number of young people looking for jobs has fallen over the last decade, the workforce is actually growing, partly because the number of women combining working with bringing up children is increasing.

Competing for jobs

Applying a simple economic equation suggests that if young people are in short supply, then their services should be in demand. However, this is not necessarily what happens, as you'll know if you're having problems getting a job. During the 1990s there was a lot of publicity about the 'demographic time-bomb', and employers were encouraged to change their traditional recruitment patterns. The net result seems to be that although fewer young people are entering the job market, it is not making it easier for them to get their first job.

Losing out to machines

The labour market is complex and lots of jobs are being superseded by machines. Take banking, for instance: those handy hole in the wall machines, which enable us to get hold of cash long after the banks have closed, mean fewer jobs for bank cashiers.

OK, so you didn't want to be a bank clerk anyway, but the principle applies in lots of industries.

HOW COMPUTERS ARE CHANGING THE WORLD

The invention of the mechanical steam engine heralded the Industrial Revolution and changed the pattern of work and life. The invention and refinement of the microchip has spearheaded another revolution with equally dramatic effects on people's lives and work.

In the future we may have robots at home which will attend to all the cleaning chores and which can be contacted by phone and given instructions: for example, told to remove a meal from the freezer, defrost it and cook it for a specific time; switch the heating and lights on and run the bath. So, it looks like there could be fewer jobs for butlers!

Supermarkets are experimenting with a whole new approach to sales and stock. In the supermarket of the future you, the customer, will pick up a bar-code scanner along with a trolley as you go through the turnstiles. Every time you add something to your trolley, you will swipe it with the scanner. This information will be electronically conveyed to the store's computer, where it will be added to your itemised bill. When you have got everything, you'll present yourself to the automated check-out where the information from the bar-code scanner will have been used to prepare the bill. So there goes another swathe of jobs.

The information about the contents of the shopper's trolley is also conveyed to the stock room so that replacement stock can be automatically prepared for an assistant to load onto the shelves. At the end of each day, the distribution warehouse (which may be hundreds of miles away) receives an automatic notification of the sales of stock from the supermarket branch. The automated stock control system instructs robots to pick and pack replacement stock to be driven to the store for opening time the next day. Want to be a lorry driver? You need to be over 21 and have an HGV licence. Maybe a fork truck licence would be useful too, but watch out because if the warehouse is modern, it will be fully automated.

Benefiting from telecommunications

Telecommunications means communicating at a distance. All around us – along telegraph wires, in cables under the high streets, by radio waves through space, by cable, by satellite, with or without wires – signals are winging their way around the world keeping people in touch and putting information at our fingertips.

Since the dawn of time the human race has been trying to find ways to communicate at a distance. It used to be smoke signals and hilltop bonfires or beacons but now it is easy to dial phone calls to the other side of the globe, to watch live television coverage of events as they happen almost anywhere in the world, to use remote controlled satellites to relay images of the weather conditions brewing up, to make phone calls from trains, planes and cars, to use the Internet to shop, bank and work from home.

Industry and commerce now routinely rely on telephones, television, radio, video-conferencing, data transmission, cable communications, alarm monitoring, faxes, telexes and remote control of instruments by telemetry.

Working from home

The developments in telecommunications mean that anyone with a computer that they can connect into the telephone network has a whole world network at their fingertips.

The Internet means that all sorts of information can be accessed from home. There's no need to go to the library: you can call up all sorts of libraries, art galleries, encyclopaedias, share prices, on-line reference material direct to your screen – as long as you have the technology and the know-how.

Telecommuting, teleworking or working from home are names given to the arrangement where employees spend some of their working week working at or from home. As information technology becomes more sophisticated and our transport systems become more and more clogged up, this is tipped to catch on!

'I am employed by a mail-order company to design their catalogues and I work from home using a computer, fax and e-mail.

I depend totally on telecommunications technology for my work. I use the phone or fax for my research, then write and design stuff on the computer. When it's ready, I plug the modem into the telephone socket and transmit the work directly from my computer through the telephone network straight to a computer at the office. I mainly use the fax to receive detailed information – maybe drawings and plans – which are too complicated to explain over the phone.

Working from home suits me very well as I live in the middle of nowhere. It is hard to find the self-discipline to work on my own, but once I'm in my office, I try to shut myself away and concentrate on work.'

Teleworker

Joining the global economy

Automation and mechanisation have replaced lots of jobs but labour costs are still a major part of any company's costs. As political and economic boundaries have come down, the economy has taken on an increasingly global aspect. Multinational companies will switch their production round the world in order to keep costs down and remain competitive. Look at the labels on household objects: where was your TV made, your washing machine, your sound system, your designer labels, your car?

And it's not just unskilled labour that is cheaper abroad. For example, one major British company subcontracts their computer programming contract to a company in southern India. The programmers there are as skilled as their British counterparts, local wage rates are much lower and the difference in time zone works to advantage. The programmers work a regular day shift maintaining and updating the software during the time when the system is quieter than during the British working day.

WHAT BASIC SKILLS WILL BE IN DEMAND?

It's guesswork, but here are some hunches. What do you think? Can you spot the trends?

Information technology

In the twenty-first century, being 'computer literate', able to use a keyboard to handle basic information via a computer, will be a fairly elementary skill required in a vast number of jobs. Whatever field you want to work in, familiarity with computers is increasingly taken for granted – a bit like being able to read and write!

The computer sections of the vacancies pages usually seem to have a fair selection of jobs. However, as the total range of systems and software is vast and expanding, if you are going to find work in this line, you need to be able to do more with computers than play games. What is needed are specialised computer skills. Traditionally, programming skills have been very much in demand. As computer programs become more sophisticated, opportunities in customising applications have arisen. In the late 1990s there was a surge in demand for skills to combat the Millennium Bug and a steady growth in vacancies for multimedia and Web programmers and designers.

However, the skills in demand now may not be in demand next year. It's a fast changing field with moving goalposts. You don't want to commit yourself to learning a particular program only to find that by the time you're trained it's gone the way of the great auk and betamax, i.e. become extinct, or it was a good idea but it never caught on. You have to research the market.

Here's a typical computer agency advertisement at the time this book goes to print (mid-1999). The demand is for skills in design, development, consultancy and support in specified systems and software. If you've got the appropriate expertise right now, you can pick and choose your placement. Maybe even name your price! On the other hand, if your skill consists of being an expert in Tomb Raiding or building Civilisations your application form will go straight in the bin.

IT & Multimedia staff required

Skills and experience required from a selection of: C/C++/ VC++, Unix, Visual Basic/VBA, NE SQL Server, Delphi, HTML, VRML, JAVA, Javascript, PERL, 3-D Image Processing, Oracle DBA. Positions include design, development, consultancy and support.

Languages

We live on the edge of a small continent where many different languages are spoken. Increasingly our business and political links with Europe are becoming closer and closer. However, fortunately for most of us, English is the main language of international trade and diplomacy. Employers in this country do like employees to have additional languages, but often it is as well as, not instead of, other specific skills. For young people in Europe the skill of speaking reading and writing another language – notably English – is an essential career tool.

'At the time I chose to do a degree in Spanish, there was a lot of talk about the career opportunities that the European Union would offer people with languages. But when I graduated I found it almost impossible to find work.

I did a number of temporary jobs and went travelling. I taught English in Spain and I worked as a courier on a Spanish camp-site. It was great fun but strictly temporary: the pay and conditions were dire but I got a great tan!

I decided to apply myself to finding a job with some career prospects. Back in London, I did a month's secretarial course which got my typing speed up to about 40 words per minute. Then I started looking for a job as a bilingual secretary. I had no idea how difficult it would be. Most employers expect bilingual secretaries to have more than one language, and they want solid secretarial skills and experience. I also had a problem justifying the number of short-term jobs I'd had and the gaps in my CV.

I did some temping work and once I actually had some experience to put on my CV, things started to get better and then I landed a job in the London branch of a Spanish Bank.

I would advise anyone interested in languages to combine business studies, marketing or law with languages. A language degree is not enough. Employers want other skills, not to mention experience. It's a good idea to get work experience at home or abroad. Even if it is voluntary work, it's something to put on the CV and that can make the difference.'

Language graduate now working in banking

Inter-personal skills

As automation takes over many routine and repetitive tasks, many of the jobs that remain revolve around dealing with people. The general term 'inter-personal skills' is used to cover the technique of being good at getting on with people; getting the best out of them be they customers, clients, colleagues or those in authority. The ability to get on with people is a vital social skill demanding tact, diplomacy, courtesy, assertiveness, firmness. It may mean managing, motivating and delegating. These nebulous, hard to define, getting-on-with-other-people skills are much in demand. They can't really be taught, but they can be learned. See the section on transferable or key skills in Chapter 3.

3

What Do Employers Want?

This is one of those 'how long is a piece of string?' questions which can only be answered with another question. So the answer to the question, 'What do employers want?' is variable and, almost by definition, not what you're offering. This chapter attempts an inventory of some of the things employers *may* want.

ATTITUDES

Definition of attitude:

A manner assumed for a specific purpose.

'You will be committed to team working, unable to take no for an answer, enjoy a fast moving and varied environment and be able to shift priorities very quickly.'

Advert for an expanding small business

'I set up my own business on a shoestring and when it started to take off I decided to take on a full-time assistant. I needed energy and enthusiasm in the business and I took on a young man who came across well at the interview and looked good on paper.

He was thorough and conscientious once he'd learnt the routine tasks. But this is a small, new business and we all have to muck in and turn our hands to whatever needs doing (preferably without waiting to be asked). He couldn't see that and whenever I asked him to put himself out – for example, to work a bit late, or deliver post by hand or tidy the office – he adopted this long-suffering air of resentment.

I don't know what the problem was – but I do not need it! I've put myself on the line to get the business going, and make jobs for other people. I expect them to show some interest and initiative.'

Owner of a small business

'Leisure is a career where there is nothing to stop someone from progressing from the bottom as long as they are prepared to move around. It's important to have a good personality and to be interested in people and to gain good recognised qualifications and experience. It's not a job for sitting back and relaxing: we have to keep the ball rolling and keep attractions coming in. We are always on the look out for new ideas.'

Sports complex manager

Attitudes quiz – Have you got an attitude?

1. *You have had a holiday job working in a shoe shop and it's your last day before you go back to college. Just your luck – an awkward customer brings back some shoes, says they don't fit and asks you for a refund. You can see that the shoes have been worn . . .*

Which of the following would you be likely to do?

a   Tell the customer to sling their hook. They are not entitled to a refund and you don't want the hassle anyway.

b   Get the manager to come and sort it out.

c   Try to explain that as the shoes have been worn, the customer is not entitled to a refund.

d   Give the customer their money back. Why not? You're leaving anyway.

2. *A young woman stops you in the street and tries to ask for directions. She speaks very little English and you find her hard to understand.*

Which of the following would you be likely to do?

a   Shrug and walk off.

b   Ask her to repeat the question slowly, and try to help her.

c   Point her confidently in one direction, then walk off in the opposite direction.

d Ask another passer-by if they can help you deal with the problem.

---

3. *Your busy sister-in-law is always moaning about the problems of getting babysitters and dog-walkers.*

Which of the following would you be likely to do?

a Go out of your way to avoid her because she is so boring.

b Offer to help her out when you've nothing better to do.

c Set up a part-time business offering babysitting and pet-sitting services in the area.

d Make anonymous phone calls, reporting her to the RSPCA and the NSPCC.

---

4. *You're slobbing around the house one afternoon when you hear the sound of brakes screeching, a loud crash and screaming. Looking out of the window you see two kids sprawled on the pavement and a car smashed into a lamppost.*

Which of the following would you be likely to do?

a Go back to watching television.

b Find your camera and go and take photographs of the scene of the accident.

c Call an ambulance then dash outside to see how you can help.

d Dash outside and start emergency first aid procedures.

---

5. *You unexpectedly win a state-of-the-art computer in a raffle.*

Which of the following would you be likely to do?

a Get the manuals out and find out how to plug in to the Internet.

b Give it away to a mate who says it's good kit.

c   Use the packed boxes as a stand for your collection of exotic empty beer bottles.

d   Put an ad in the local paper and sell it for what you can get.

6. *An elderly relative asks you to change the plug on an electrical fire. While you are doing this you realise that the cable is badly frayed and you think that the fire is dangerous.*

Which of the following would you be likely to do?

a   Explain the problem and take the fire home to repair.

b   Change the plug and tell your relative not to use it until it's been repaired.

c   Decide it's not your problem, say nothing, change the plug and go home.

d   Leave the fire as it is and say nothing. It's impossible to explain things to your relative.

7. *You're at a party and two of your friends get into a very heated argument. This has happened before and you know that if you intervene you might be able to calm them down.*

Which of the following would you be likely to do?

a   Leave the party – it's so embarrassing to be associated with them.

b   Stride into the fray telling them both to back off, and try to defuse the situation.

c   Go and get yourself another drink and find someone new to chat up.

d   Egg them on, giving a running commentary on who's going to strike the first blow.

8. *One of your friends is planning to undertake a sponsored bike ride from John o'Groats to Lands End to raise money for a local good cause.*

Which of the following would you be likely to do?

a   Wish them good luck and offer to sponsor them for a couple of quid.

b   Offer to help out in any way you can – by training with them or helping with publicity.

c   Tell yourself that this friend is quite insane and avoid them until after the event.

d   Warn the friend that cycling is a dangerous and anti-social activity and they run a serious risk of making themselves a laughing stock.

Attitudes analysis
For each answer you chose, give yourself points as follows:

1. a=1; b=4, c=5; d=2
2. a=2; b=5; c=1; d=4
3. a=2, b=3; c=5; d=1
4. a=1; b=2; c=4; d=5
5. a=5; b=2; c=1; d=3
6. a=5; b=4; c=2; d=1
7. a=1; b=5; c=2; d=3
8. a=3; b=5; c=1; d=1

Then add up your total score and find out how you rate on the attitude test.

Total 32–40
Lots of brownie points for you. Sounds like you've got a good attitude and are prepared to take responsibility for events and act on your own initiative. Give yourself a big pat on the back (NB the publishers can accept no responsibility for the osteopath's bill).

Total 17–31
You respond constructively to some situations, but not to others. You can afford to be more confident about your ability to deal with situations and solve problems.

Total 8–16
Sounds like you have a lot of fun – usually at someone else's expense. It seems like you can't be bothered to put yourself out for anyone. You're not exactly the answer to an employer's prayer!

Motivation
Employers emphatically want people with motivation. What is motivation? The word is now in common use, but that is a fairly recent development. Can you find it in a dictionary? Surprisingly, it's missing from older, more traditional dictionaries. I tracked down a couple of references to it: one says it's a vogue word which may not become established. Another says it's a word employed by psychologists and educational psychologists and best left to them!

Too late, because it's entered the collection of jargon and phrases that are part of the employment business. So, what is motivation?

Motivation – *that which motivates, makes move or happen.*
Motivate – *to cause to feel an active interest.*

Motivation and self-motivation are prized qualities because they mean that someone has the internal drive and belief that goes with getting things done: making decisions, acting on them and seeing things through.

YOUR CAPABILITIES AND SKILLS
It's an employers' market. The supply of jobhunters exceeds the demand for them. One response to this situation is that extra hoops have been introduced for jobseekers to jump through. During the 1980s a whole new set of skills and capabilities were introduced to the vocabulary of the Personnel Department and the vocational education curriculum.

These skills include the collection of capabilities which allow people to succeed in a wide range of different tasks and jobs. They include effective communication, negotiation skills, problem-solving ability, working as a member of a team, numeracy, and the ability to adapt to new and changing situations. They are characterised by a resourceful approach to tasks and are a product of applying experience and education.

Definition of capable – *a feature or faculty capable of development*.
Definition of skills – *developed aptitudes or ability in particular fields*.

Transferable skills
This term is used to describe capabilities which allow people to succeed in a wide range of different tasks and jobs. They can include:

Group work skills.
The ability to work with others towards a common aim; an appreciation of the importance of team-building and of different roles within groups in accomplishing organisational objectives.

Problem-solving skills.
The ability to define and solve complex problems within time, manpower and financial constraints.

Achieving results.
The ability to recognise opportunities, appraise needs, evaluate risks and execute effective action plans.

Personal effectiveness.
The qualities and skills possessed by the resourceful individual.

Your communication skills

Verbal skills.
The ability to speak to a point and communicate a specific message, series of facts or arguments; assessing audience awareness and responding to feedback.

Written skills.
The ability to write simple, focused text with a clearly defined purpose which can be understood by the intended audience.

Numeracy
- The ability to work with numbers and to use them to analyse and express facts.

- Ability to carry out basic calculations, handle figures, gather and process data.

Computer literacy
- The ability to use computers as an aid to writing and numeracy skills and to get access to reference material.

Enterprise

Enterprise is another one of those buzz-words much in vogue during recent years. Being enterprising is considered an asset in the world of commerce and industry. So what does enterprise mean? Some alternative definitions are:

The wish, power and ability to begin and follow through a plan or task.

An exciting, often hazardous undertaking.

Something undertaken, especially requiring extensive planning and work.

Most people would agree that the enterprising person is resourceful, adaptable, creative, innovative and dynamic and has the qualities and skills which enable people to succeed in business.

'COMPUTING HELP DESK ANALYSTS
We are looking for people with a good working knowledge of MS Office, Excel, Powerpoint and Word for an exciting new project.

If you enjoy helping people and you are energetic and reliable with a flexible attitude, good telephone manner and keyboard skills then we want to hear from you.

If you have what it takes to work in a customer orientated environment then contact us.'

Agency advertisement

'The only reason I got the job is because I can use a word processor and presentation package. I don't plan to stay as a

PA but it's got my foot in the door and it's giving me experience.'

Languages graduate

'All the staff here have to be able to cover all the jobs: selling tickets, doing the bar and café, running the games and maintaining and repairing the kit. When I interview, I'm looking for an outgoing personality and common sense. A background in electronics, awareness of safety considerations and first aid qualifications are all an advantage. It helps to have played the game, but I avoid employing keen players.

You need to be able to stand up in front of 20 customers and explain the game with the authority to get the rules across and stress that it is only a game. Supervising a game, and making sure it's played safely takes common sense and maturity. If a game gets out of hand, the Marshall can use remote control to terminate the offender's pack. No pack – no fun!

The weekends are our busy times. I try to arrange things so that people can get time off when they want, but staff all have to be flexible about the hours they work. Staff get a bonus if we do well, so it's in everyone's interests to keep customers coming in. We use a marketing agency for publicity, but all the staff here try and come up with ideas for boosting business.'

Manager of a laser game complex talking about staff
recruitment

Are you a go-getting whizz-kid?

Maybe you're cut out for life as an entrepreneur. Consider the statements in the quiz on page 38 and for each of them, tick the box that is appropriate to you. You might find it interesting to ask someone who knows you well to complete the quiz about you.

YOUR QUALIFICATIONS

Most people going through school or college are encouraged to think that getting qualifications is very important: that examination success is the gateway to a good career. Good results can certainly help, particularly for people starting on the job hunt, but they are not the be all and end all and some employers have a slightly ambivalent attitude to qualifications.

	Always	Usually	Sometimes	Never
I've got the energy to keep working long hours if necessary	_____	_____	_____	_____
I am good at getting things done	_____	_____	_____	_____
I can make long-term commitments and work towards distant goals	_____	_____	_____	_____
I'm motivated by the prospect of making money	_____	_____	_____	_____
I like to solve problems	_____	_____	_____	_____
I set myself challenging but achievable goals	_____	_____	_____	_____
I analyse situations and come up with solutions to problems	_____	_____	_____	_____
I'll take calculated risks	_____	_____	_____	_____
If I make mistakes I can learn from them	_____	_____	_____	_____
I know when to seek advice	_____	_____	_____	_____
I can cope with stress	_____	_____	_____	_____
I can handle uncertain situations	_____	_____	_____	_____
I set myself high standards and make sure I meet them	_____	_____	_____	_____
I can think on my feet to adapt to fast-moving situations	_____	_____	_____	_____
I have a high degree of commitment to any project I'm involved with	_____	_____	_____	_____
I take personal responsibility for tasks I commit myself to	_____	_____	_____	_____
I look for creative and innovative solutions to problems	_____	_____	_____	_____
I can motivate others	_____	_____	_____	_____
I've got good management skills	_____	_____	_____	_____
I'm a good organiser	_____	_____	_____	_____
I can be assertive without being aggressive	_____	_____	_____	_____
I take a positive approach to things I'm involved in	_____	_____	_____	_____

If your ticks are clustered at the left-hand side of the table, then you may have the qualities it takes to be your own boss. If your ticks accumulate on the right-hand side, then working for someone else is going to be rather more your style – as soon as you can track down that elusive first job.

Good qualifications can offer vital evidence of a candidate's suitability, but some employers are cynical about qualifications and look for different qualities. This is most likely to apply to small businesses where the boss prides him/herself on qualifying in the 'University of Life' or 'School of Hard Knocks'.

As people get older and have more experience to offer, qualifications may become less important in securing a job.

If you don't have qualifications, you may be in good company: John Major is notoriously bashful about his decidedly modest O level record, yet that didn't stop him becoming Prime Minister.

New qualifications

Most employers are familiar with the mainstream school and college qualifications: GCSE, A levels, degrees and HND are well-established, but some others – particularly the newer ones – are less well-established. This includes A/S levels, and General, Scottish and National Vocational Qualifications. These new vocational awards – NVQs/SVQs/GNVQs – are work-related qualifications which are designed to tell employers that the holder has specific job skills.

Like any new qualifications, it may take a while for them to become accepted and recognised. If you've done S/NVQs or GNVQs be prepared to explain (concisely and positively) what they are and what you learned.

For further information see Appendix 2 on vocational qualifications.

Too qualified?

While having good qualifications is necessary for some jobs, for others it may be considered downright unhelpful. Just as qualifications are considered to show that the candidate has the potential to go far, they may also indicate (particularly in the case of routine and menial jobs) that the candidate will not be satisfied in the job: after a while they will find the job boring and are likely to be discontented and move on. That's fine if there are opportunities for advancement within the company but if not, then the employer may be looking for a plodder who likes a steady routine.

If you are applying for a job where your qualifications considerably exceed the minimum required, think carefully about how to handle this. You may need to find a way of presenting yourself to reassure the employer that you will take the job seriously.

'I applied for a job with a paint company, as a technician testing paints. As I've just finished a degree in chemistry, I thought I was in with a good chance. I got as far as the interview but I discovered that good qualifications can be a drawback. The company had advertised for someone with one A level and they thought that I was overqualified for the job and wouldn't stick at it. The second thing that counted against me was not having any work experience. They didn't offer me the job and I'm still searching.'

Unemployed chemistry graduate

'I did a course in film studies at college and got involved in lots of film-making projects. My ambition was to be a film director, so when the course finished I applied for loads of production jobs. Me and thousands of others I think.

All the while I had a part-time job at a local multiplex cinema selling popcorn and ice cream. After six months, I had to re-think. My boss at the multiplex asked me if I'd like to go full-time as a trainee manager. I reluctantly took the job. Since I started I've really got into it and although the hours are very anti-social, I'm enjoying the management side of cinema.'

Trainee manager, multiplex cinema

YOUR POTENTIAL

Dictionary definition of potential:

Something that can develop or become actual.

Every one of us has got potential, although unfortunately a lot of people don't realise it. It's important to believe in yourself and your ability. Self-development doesn't end when you leave education: there's lots more to learn and it's a fascinating process.

Learning

We are all born full of curiosity and with an innate ability to learn. From the moment we enter the world we are on a voyage of discovery, mastering physical and mental skills and trying to understand the world around us.

In the first years of our lives, we humans learn at an amazing rate. Within the space of a few years we learn to walk, talk, live as a member of a community and control all manner of sophisticated gadgets. As we get older the rate at which we learn slows down, but that's only by comparison with the phenomenal rate of our early development. Anyone with the necessary interest and enthusiasm can carry on learning and developing throughout their life.

Self-development

Every one of us is full of potential and the way we make the most of ourselves is through self-development. Acquiring new skills, knowledge, attitudes and understanding means exploring your potential and making the most of your situation. Self-development is a stimulating and rewarding process which increases self-confidence and ability to take control of life.

'Taking on school and college leavers is a bit like laying down fine wines. You do your best to assess what they are like at the moment, and then try to anticipate which ones will mature well to give you real value for money in the future. It's a gamble.'

Personnel officer, multinational company

'When we take on management trainees, we look at their qualifications to give us an indication of potential. We don't expect trainees to bring specific work skills to the organisation, as we run a planned training scheme where they gain hands-on experience of every aspect of the company's operation. What we look for is enthusiasm, ability to get on well with people and a readiness to roll up their sleeves and do the job.'

Personnel manager, leisure company

'You will be an aware and articulate communicator with high self-esteem and good grooming. Ideally your degree will be science or technology based, but your attitude and desire to excel are of most importance to us, and an arts degree matched with determination to succeed in the commercial world is acceptable. Maturity is more important than experience, and common sense will rate highly. You will also have the following characteristics: integrity, drive, ambition and above all will know what you want out of life.'

Advertisement for trainee account executives

'Have you got what it takes to build a career in sales with us? You must be a graduate or well educated with a business qualification. In your early twenties, completely mobile within the UK, and have a full clean driving licence. You may have already made your mark in sales or had some experience in the commercial sector; if not don't worry as it is less important than an enthusiastic and outgoing personality with strong self-motivation and good organisational skills, plus your commitment to a sales career.'

Advertisement for graduate sales reps

'We mainly recruit by word of mouth. If necessary we use the Jobcentre. We take on unskilled and unqualified staff and train them on the job. There are lots of opportunities for keen people to work their way up. For example, our second chef started with us a couple of years ago as a kitchen porter. Now he's qualified and ready for promotion.

When people come for interviews, I look for enthusiasm and the ability to get on with people. Experience helps, but it is not necessary. Being clean and presentable is essential.

We always start people on a trial period. Sometimes it is clear on the first day that they are not cut out for the business. We tell them right away – at least they get paid for their trial.'

Manager, four star hotel

YOUR APPEARANCE

There's an old saying, 'you can't judge a book by its cover'. Yet many people pride themselves on the ability to judge someone's personality and character by their appearance.

How do you feel about judging and being judged in this way? How important do you think appearance is? What does someone's appearance tell you about them? Do you think that you can tell someone's character and personality by their appearance? Is your appearance a good guide to your inner self?

First impressions

Research has shown that we form lasting impressions within the first couple of minutes of meeting new people. People form 90 per cent of their opinion within a minute and a half of the first meeting. Subsequent meetings and conversations may make them change their mind, but it can be an uphill struggle to get them to modify first impressions.

Psychologists' research into the impression people make on the first meeting has come up with the following analysis:

- 55 per cent of the impression is determined by what they *see*. This includes colouring, appearance, posture, body language, facial expression and eye contact.

- 38 per cent of the impression is determined by what they *hear*. This includes tone, pace and pitch of the voice, pauses and hesitations, clarity of speech, accent.

- 7 per cent of the impression is determined by the *words* they hear.

This means that what someone looks and sounds like makes much more of an impression than what they actually say.

So, if you are going to an interview, or going cold-calling, it's worth thinking carefully about the messages your appearance and non-verbal communication give!

If the first contact is talking to someone on the phone, then the words will be more significant, but tone, pace and pitch of the voice, pauses and hesitations and accent will all influence the impression made.

A tip for telephoning: if you're talking to someone on the telephone, try and smile as you talk because although unseen, the timbre and tone of the voice are much warmer when the face forms a smile! If you don't believe this, experiment on your friends and see if they notice.

For more information about body language see the section in Chapter 8 on non-verbal communication.

Image

The growth of massive world-wide media coverage has led to a new industry: the image consultant. Lots of people in the public eye – pop groups, film stars, politicians, royalty – employ image consultants to help groom their image to court public popularity.

Image consultants advise on a whole range of matters: style, colour, cut and type of clothes; make up, jewellery, fragrance; accessories, what to say, how to say it; who to talk to; who not to talk to; where to be seen and with whom. Image is not just appearance, it is the sum of the signals sent out by appearance, body language and speech.

Clothes, accessories, hairstyle and body decoration (tattoos and piercing) are a personal statement: a statement by individuals about who they are. However, people have very different interpretations of image. Clothes and accessories that are seen as very fashionable by one group of people may send a quite different message to another group.

What do employers look for?
Everyone agrees that being clean and tidy is essential. However, the images employers want their staff to project are diverse. There are some careers where it is a positive advantage to look very fashion conscious and trendy. Industries where this applies include design, music, hair and fashion. In others areas – the financial world, banking, etc. – a traditional image conveying security and respectability is important.

Appearing at an interview
There is a lot of debate about what it is appropriate to wear for an interview. Some people say you should dress as you would for the job. Others say that it is better to dress up for an interview. There are no hard and fast rules about this. It is a good idea to find out what the 'dress codes' for the job are, and to aim for an appearance that is at the smart end of this.

Different standards apply in different jobs and industries. In some jobs, style of dress is of little significance. In others it is important and uniforms may be provided for employees to wear.

Clean, tidy and well-groomed is the order of the day. Whatever you decide to wear, be sure that you are comfortable wearing the outfit. There's nothing worse than shoes that don't fit or clothes you feel ill at ease wearing.

'Our best stylists are trained in the salon. It's a two-year apprenticeship with day release at college. Lately we have had problems keeping apprentices. That's partly because the wages are low, but also because school-leavers come with unrealistic expectations: they think they can be unleashed on customers' hair right away, whereas they spend their first months learning about the salon, and doing general clearing up.

When interviewing we look for someone with a bit of style, fashion-conscious and obviously interested in hair.

Qualifications are fairly secondary. What's more important is to get on well with people. Being able to talk to customers is a very important part of the job.'

Hair salon manageress

YOUR EXPERIENCE

Employers want experience, but if you are looking for your first job you haven't got any experience. Without experience you can't get a job; without a job you can't get experience. It's Catch 22.

Why do they want experience?
Broadly speaking, employers find it reassuring to employ people with experience because there is more chance that they will be accustomed to the routine and rules of the workplace and settle into a new job.

One complaint frequently heard from employers is that when school-leavers start work, they don't understand the importance of getting things right every time. At school eight out of ten in maths was a pretty good mark. At work, every calculation has to be right and people are trusted to get the answers without having them corrected every time. People with experience of work are likely to understand this.

What other differences are there between working and being a student?

How to make the most of your experience
If you've recently left school or college and are looking for your first job you need to make an inventory of your hobbies, voluntary work and part-time work. Then sort out what experience you want to emphasise to make yourself sound like an enterprising, responsible and eminently desirable prospective employee. (See the box on page 46.)

Another example
If you're planning to return to work, having spent the last few years running a household and bringing up two children single-handed, never mind 'I'm only a parent', your responsibilities have included:

• full-time management of a unit of three people

Jobs I have had	Job skills I did well	Hidden skills I demonstrated
Newspaper round	Delivering papers Collecting cash Organising the round Memorising the round	Getting up early Being friendly to customers Coping with bad Keeping my bike in good order
Checkout operator	Scanning in bar codes Keying in codes and totals Taking customers' cash Giving correct change Doing credit card transactions	Being friendly to customers Concentrating throughout shift Getting on with workmates Time-keeping

- catering

- cooking

- cleaning

- budgeting

- planning

- administering

- providing support, counselling, arbitration, conciliation and first aid.

Volunteering for experience

Voluntary work can give you:

- new skills

- experience

- a sense of purpose

- training

- satisfaction of contributing to the community.

If you are unemployed and you think lack of experience is a problem, you can do something about it. Voluntary work is a good way of getting a toe-hold in the job market, of gaining new skills or brushing up old ones. Volunteering can be a chance to gain new skills, interests and experience, use your existing skills and expertise, get training, meet people and make a difference in the community.

Volunteers are in demand for a huge range of tasks: conservation work, hospital radio, working with children, working with animals, taking on counselling or advice work, driving, decorating, gardening and working in charities' shops and offices. National Parks, museums, art galleries, charities, schools, playgroups and drop-in centres all rely on volunteers to help them keep going.

To get ideas about what is available in your area, drop in at your local volunteer bureau for a chat, look on the notice board in the library, or ask at a local community centre or Citizens Advice Bureau.

4

How Do You Measure Up?

Well, we've looked at the employers' wish-list and now we know what they want. Someone with a brilliant brain, the patience of a saint, the foresight of a clairvoyant, the insight of a trained counsellor, loads of experience, nicely turned out, positive outgoing personality and prepared to work cheerfully for a pittance.

A tall order, you might think. Hard to measure up to this pen-picture of a paragon. Well, that's OK because we know the world is not flawless, and actually such perfection does not really exist.

THINKING POSITIVELY

'Whether you think you can or you can't, you're probably right.'

Henry Ford

Being positive about yourself is vital. If you don't feel good about yourself, why should anyone else? However, that positive attitude can become victim to a spiral of despair. A vicious circle sets in when we feel low. Our self-confidence takes a knock making it very hard to feel good about ourselves. But without confidence and a positive self-image, it's even harder to take the steps which might start to turn the situation around and get us out of the slough of despond and negative thinking.

Knowing your own strengths

You have to have confidence in yourself. Whatever happens, you have the right to take charge of your life – and that means feeling positive about yourself. Fundamental to feeling good about yourself is having a good self-image. This means recognising and valuing your own strengths, skills and qualities. Part of the knack of feeling positive about yourself lies in developing and projecting self-confidence. If you are someone who tends to under-rate or play down your skills and capabilities, it may be time to start changing the way you think about yourself.

Building self-confidence

A lot of sports coaches responsible for motivating and training top athletes have adopted the 'Inner Game' approach. This means building up self-confidence so that it becomes a feature of the personality. Self-confidence alone is not enough to make anyone successful, but without confidence, success is likely to remain elusive.

An important part of the technique is to instil the belief that 'you can if you think you can'. As most of us don't have a professional coach looking after our psychological and physical well-being, we have to find ways of doing this for ourselves.

Creative visualisation

There are books about the Inner Dialogue and Inner Game, explaining how it is done. Part of the technique involves something called 'creative visualisation'. Athletes or sportsmen are trained to run through their competition event in the mind's eye. They repeat this 'action preview' a number of times, always making sure that they finish in first place in fine style.

It has been established that far from being a waste of time, day-dreaming, when used constructively, can make a very positive contribution to people's attitude and self-confidence.

Accentuating the positive

Write ten incredibly positive statements about yourself. Pick out qualities that you possess and be very up-beat about yourself. For example:

I am reliable.
I am trustworthy.
I am a good listener.
I keep a cool head in a crisis.
I am good at negotiating solutions to problems at home.

. . . .
. . . .
. . . .
. . . .
. . . .

. . . .
. . . .
. . . .
. . . .
. . . .

If you find this difficult, ask your friends and family for help, but stress to them that you want them to concentrate on being incredibly positive about you! If it helps set the mood you could do the same for them.

DEVELOPING SELF-CONFIDENCE

Being self-confident means feeling good about yourself: having a positive image of yourself. It's not a skill, but a set of feelings – an attitude of mind. You can tell when people are confident: their shoulders are back, they walk tall, look the world in the eye, believe in themselves, feel they have the right to their own opinions and to express them.

It's easier to see self-confidence in other people than in ourselves. It's clear to us when other people are brimming with confidence. What's less clear is why they feel that way, or even whether their confidence is genuine or a well-rehearsed act.

What makes people self-confident?

Confidence is about two things: how you feel about yourself and how you feel about situations you expect to be in. To feel confident, you need to:

- feel that other people respect and value you

- feel able to communicate, understand and be understood

- understand the situations you find yourself in

- feel you have the skills and knowledge to handle these situations.

Building confidence

One technique for building confidence, as mentioned earlier, is creative visualisation. It is used in a variety of situations from holistic health treatment to sports psychology and interview preparation.

It is rather like day-dreaming, except that you take on the role of director and make sure that the 'dream' or creative visualisation follows a carefully constructed plot. You are the writer as well as the director. There's no guarantee that it will work, but it's a pleasant way to while away time and if you get the script right, it'll leave you feeling more positive about yourself.

You can try it with all sorts of things. It involves letting your mind's eye and imagination loose on a forthcoming event. Construct the scenario and let your mind's eye be the camera, showing you what happens. It's vital that you are the hero of the story: that you look good, sound good and conduct yourself with confidence and aplomb. Remember you are in charge so make sure you are the hero of the day.

Self-perception questionnaires

Recognising and identifying your own strengths can be difficult. In our culture it is considered brash or arrogant to be too self-confident. People who are diffident and modest are much readier to identify their weaknesses. However, that won't do – you've got to be clear about your strengths and ready to use them to advantage. Use the personality and skills rating chart on page 52 to assess your own strengths.

It can be interesting also to get someone who knows you to complete the assessment about you. Is there much of a difference between the way others see you and the way you see yourself?

Another interesting variation is to complete the rating for yourself as you are in different situations. For instance, you may behave in quite different ways at home, at school, at work, with friends and on holiday.

RECOGNISING YOUR STRENGTHS

With unemployment high and rising, it's an employers' market. This means that most job vacancies have lots of people chasing them. If you are going to be the one who succeeds, it's important to present yourself well – in person, on the phone and on paper. This doesn't mean boasting or telling lies, but it does mean working on positive presentation of your personality, skills and experience, and taking an up-beat and confident approach when you're letting employers know what you can offer.

Estate agents and car salesmen are well-known for their creative use of the English language – we've all seen their adverts. Why not try writing a short advertisement for yourself? Remember, the idea is to present yourself in a very positive light without lying! Even better, get some friends to join in and write advertisements for each other.

Personality and skills rating

Put a ring round the point which represents your personality. For example, if you think you are well-organised, mark 2 on the scale.

Well-organised	1 2 3 4 5 6	. . . Confused
Calm	1 2 3 4 5 6	. . . Excitable
Reliable	1 2 3 4 5 6	. . . Unpredictable
Industrious	1 2 3 4 5 6	. . . Casual
Quick-witted	1 2 3 4 5 6	. . . Slow to learn
Trustworthy	1 2 3 4 5 6	. . . Devious
Consistent	1 2 3 4 5 6	. . . Moody
Relaxed	1 2 3 4 5 6	. . . Highly strung
Self-confident	1 2 3 4 5 6	. . . Self-effacing
Even-tempered	1 2 3 4 5 6	. . . Quick-tempered
Creative	1 2 3 4 5 6	. . . Conformist
Tactful	1 2 3 4 5 6	. . . Forthright
Ambitious	1 2 3 4 5 6	. . . Unassuming
Bossy	1 2 3 4 5 6	. . . Subservient
Risk-taker	1 2 3 4 5 6	. . . Cautious
Persuasive	1 2 3 4 5 6	. . . Inarticulate
Patient	1 2 3 4 5 6	. . . Impatient
Well-groomed	1 2 3 4 5 6	. . . Casually dressed
Tolerant	1 2 3 4 5 6	. . . Intolerant

Listing your skills

If you lack confidence in your abilities, try listing things you've done recently which you've been proud of. It might be dealing with people in difficult situations, it might be coping coolly in a crisis, it might be succeeding against the odds. Then extend this by thinking about other characteristics that could develop out of these skills and interests. If natural modesty makes it hard for you

Self-assessment – social skills

Use this self-assessment to identify your strengths and boost your confidence. If you identify weaknesses, then start thinking about practical ways in which you can start changing things.

I find . . .	*Very difficult*	*Not at all difficult*
Dealing with authority	3 2 1	1 2 3
Doing the things I want to do	3 2 1	1 2 3
Feeling good about myself	3 2 1	1 2 3
Being self-confident	3 2 1	1 2 3
Making decisions	3 2 1	1 2 3
The way other people treat me	3 2 1	1 2 3
Treating other people fairly	3 2 1	1 2 3
Controlling my temper	3 2 1	1 2 3
Coping with feelings of depression	3 2 1	1 2 3
Feeling isolated	3 2 1	1 2 3
Finding job vacancies	3 2 1	1 2 3
Filling in forms	3 2 1	1 2 3
Using the telephone	3 2 1	1 2 3
Being interviewed for a job	3 2 1	1 2 3
Getting a job	3 2 1	1 2 3
Keeping a job	3 2 1	1 2 3
Making a good impression	3 2 1	1 2 3
Getting information I need	3 2 1	1 2 3
Managing money	3 2 1	1 2 3
Having time on my hands	3 2 1	1 2 3

Situation	Challenge	Qualities and skills needed
In a busy street, I saw someone snatch an old lady's handbag.	*To stop thief, and restore the gag to the owner.*	*A loud, confident and authoritative voice to frighten the theif into dropping the bag.*
In the pub with a group of mates, Martin had drunk too much and was upsetting people.	*To coax him into leaving the put and going home quietly.*	*Tact and diplomacy firmness*
Trying to do a group project at college with other students who could not be bothered.	*To persuade them that it was worth doing, and doing well.*	*Leadership, organisation, lateral thinking.*
A group of kids were bulling a Year 8 kid who was in tears.	*To shame them into stopping because they they knew they were behaving badly.*	*Confidence, logic, powers of persuasion.*

Situation	Challenge	Qualities and skills needed

to do this, ask your friends and family where they think your talents lie.

To help alert you to the number of both obvious and 'hidden skills', try analysing projects you've been involved in and extract the skills you needed to carry them out. Be honest but don't be bashful. Include a list of the skills you use in coping with everyday situations as well as the more challenging moments.

Look at the examples opposite, and then complete the blank grid for yourself.

BEHAVING ASSERTIVELY

Part of being self-confident and projecting well is the ability to behave assertively in all sorts of situations. Being assertive means communicating your needs, wishes and feelings clearly and directly to other people. People who behave assertively feel good about themselves and their behaviour.

When people behave assertively they:

- Make it clear what they expect from other people.

- Express their feelings honestly.

- Stay calm and relaxed in difficult situations.

- Give and accept fair criticisms.

- Give and accept sincere compliments.

- Treat other people as they would like to be treated themselves.

When people behave assertively they *do not*:

- Try to bully or manipulate others into doing things against their will.

- Allow themselves to be bullied or manipulated by other people.

- Get aggressive or upset in disagreements with others.

Behaving assertively is quite different from being aggressive. It's an important life skill and one that can take quite a lot of practice. It's worth it though!

Role models
Culture and gender often mean we learn particular types of behaviour from an early age.

Some people are encouraged to:	*Others are encouraged to:*
be tough and strong	be gentle
take the lead	follow
be in control	be compassionate
not back down	put others before themselves
give as good as they get	share
show no weakness	not argue
win, whatever the cost	not get angry

Do you agree with this observation? Who do you think are the two groups of people?

Being aggressive or being passive
It is a generalisation to say that these stereotypes lead to aggressive behaviour on the one hand and passive behaviour on the other. However, it is widely believed that women find it difficult to assert themselves, while men find it difficult to express their feelings. Aggressive behaviour is based on a belief that life is a battle or a competition and the way to come out on top is to be the winner. Essentially, an aggressive approach to winning means that there are going to be losers. Passive behaviour involves always putting the needs of others first, regardless of the inconvenience or personal sacrifice involved.

Changing your ways
However, it doesn't have to be like that. Neither of these sets of attitudes and behaviour is a recipe for successful and happy ways of dealing with people. Aggressive behaviour intimidates and upsets others. Passive behaviour leads to resentment and unhappiness. Dealing effectively and successfully with others demands negotiation, compromise and the ability to listen.

Assertive behaviour is based on being straightforward and honest, letting people know where they stand with you. Assertiveness depends on the ability and willingness to evaluate, communicate and negotiate. At its best it leads to win-win situations between people. It is a mature and adult way to behave.

Practical tips for assertive behaviour

Three logical steps lead to assertive behaviour:

1. Actively listen to what is being said to you. Let the other person know that you hear and understand what they are saying (use body language and other non-verbal messages).

2. Say what you think and feel in a direct way.

3. Say clearly what you want to happen.

Developing your assertion techniques

Broken record
If you have to deal with people who won't (or don't want to) listen, try using the broken record technique. Simply repeat what you want to say in a calm and thoughtful way until it gets through. The key is to keep repeating your message until it is no longer ignored or dismissed. It is a good idea to use some of the phrases over and over again in different sentences. This gets the message home and prevents others from distracting you or throwing in red herrings.

Fogging
Some people have an unfortunate tendency to approach others very aggressively. This usually provokes either aggression or defensiveness. Fogging is a technique for dealing with anger or aggression by disarming it. If you can do it, fogging will stop manipulative criticism while still protecting your self-esteem.

   Here are some examples of an aggressive approach, disarmed by fogging. On each occasion the criticism is acknowledged, but it is diminished and brought into perspective as a criticism of one specific event, rather than accepted as an across-the-board condemnation.

Goad: I admire your nerve, wearing that outfit for an interview.

Response:	You may be right, perhaps it is not appropriate for a formal occasion.
Goad:	You are the most inconsiderate person I've ever met.
Response:	It's true that I can be selfish – but there are times when I have to put myself first.
Goad:	You are impossible – why do you always turn everything into such a pig-sty?
Response:	I know my untidiness annoys you, but it is my room.

Dealing with problem areas

Saying no
Sometimes refusing a request can be difficult. However, if you end up agreeing to do something you really didn't want to it can lead to feelings of annoyance, impatience, dissatisfaction, etc. It is better to say clearly and directly that you do not want to do something, rather than make excuses, long-winded apologies or tell elaborate lies.

Remember, when you say no you are refusing the request, not rejecting the person. If you are not ready to make a decision, respond by asking for more information or say you need time to think about it. Above all, don't be manipulated into feeling guilty for refusing a request.

Receiving compliments
Learn to accept compliments. If someone gives you a compliment, enjoy it – don't try and dismiss it.

Giving criticism
People can get hooked on being critical: giving criticism. It's easy to lose sight of the fact that criticism should be constructive, with the emphasis on how to get things right in future rather than what has gone wrong in the past.

Whether giving or receiving criticism try and separate it from the person – it's a criticism of something that happened, not a wholesale assault on someone's personality.

Aggressive, assertive or passive?

Behaving assertively means finding a balance between aggression on the one hand and passive behaviour on the other.

Aggression	= fight
Assertion	= discuss, negotiate, argue
Passivity	= flight

How these attitudes come across is compared in the table below. Are there other characteristics you can add to the list?

	Assertive	**Aggressive**	**Passive**
Posture	Upright or straight	Leaning forward	Shrinking, hunched shoulders
Head	Firm, relaxed	Jutting chin, clenched jaw	Head down
Eyes	Regular eye contact without staring	Staring, piercing or glaring eye contact	Little eye contact, averted gaze
Voice	Calm and well-modulated	Shouting, loud, emphatic	Whining, hesitant, mumbling
Face	Expressive	Set and firm	Smiling, even when upset
Hands	Relaxed gestures	Pointing, jabbing fingers, sharp gestures	Hand wringing

How assertive are you?

Answer the 10 questions on pages 60–1, marking the answer which most accurately describes your typical response. Then go back through the questionnaire and mark the answer which describes how you would like to behave.

1. *In a new situation, if I am unsure of something*:
   I can easily ask for help.
   I get embarrassed and apologetic.
   I get exasperated.

2. *If I'm asked my opinion about something*:
   I try and say what I think people want to hear.
   I feel comfortable saying what I think, even if I know it won't be popular.
   I find I often express myself very forcefully.

3. *If I'm given faulty goods in a shop*:
   I find it very difficult to complain.
   I complain, but usually end up having a slanging match.
   I can state my case without attacking the other person.

4. *If I think I'm being taken for granted*:
   I feel like a doormat and sulk.
   I get furious and have a row.
   I try and discuss what is happening, in order to make changes.

5. *If I am criticised deservedly*:
   I feel terrible.
   I get angry.
   I accept the criticism of my behaviour, knowing it is not the end of the world.

6. *If someone makes a complaint which is unfair and aggressive*:
   I get angry and shout back.
   I listen quietly but get angry afterwards.
   I handle the situation by discussing it coolly.

7. *When someone is sarcastic at my expense*:
   I get upset.
   I respond with angry sarcasm.
   I point out to them that they are behaving in an unnecessary and hurtful way.

8. *If I am being put down or patronised*:
   I get very hot under the collar.
   I feel very inadequate.
   I raise the issue without being aggressive.

9. *If I think someone has done something well*:
   I find it easy to compliment them.
   I find it embarrassing to praise people.
   It sounds hollow if I try and give compliments.

10. *If I am being given the run-around by someone in authority*:
   I get angry, bluster at them, then flounce out in a fury.
   I let them push me around then go home angrily.
   I stand my ground and repeat my case in a cool and confident manner.

Once you have worked your way through the quiz go back over it and work out which responses are assertive, which aggressive and which are passive.

What practical steps can you take so that you respond in the way that you would like to behave?

CAN YOU BE RELIED UPON?

Complete the reliability quiz on page 62 for yourself. Then get someone who knows you well to answer each of the questions about you.

Is there a lot of difference between their assessment and your self-assessment? If so, what does this tell you about yourself?

HOW FLEXIBLE ARE YOU?

Complete the flexibility quiz on page 63. Do you think you are flexible and open-minded? What advantages and disadvantages does this have? How can you present this to your best advantage?

CHECKING YOUR SELF-PRESENTATION

Get some paper and a pen and make a list of what you think an employer wants. Then note down alongside each item how you think you rate.

The next problem is to think of how to present these qualities to a prospective employer. Initially, you usually have to find a way of putting them across on paper. Rather than claiming 'I am flexible, adaptable, open-minded and creative', it is better to express this in the context of relevant experience.

Reliability quiz

	Always	Usually	Sometimes	Never
If I agree to do something, I'll carry it through	_____	_____	_____	_____
If I arrange a rendezvous, I'll be on time	_____	_____	_____	_____
If I spot something that needs doing, even if it's not my responsibility, I'll see it gets done	_____	_____	_____	_____
If I'm driving, I stick to my resolve not to drink alcohol	_____	_____	_____	_____
If I have an unpleasant task, I'll do it	_____	_____	_____	_____
If I've promised not to do something, I'll stick to my word, even if it means a loss of street credibility	_____	_____	_____	_____
I make realistic estimates of how long it will take me to do something	_____	_____	_____	_____
I keep my overdraft and credit card within my limits	_____	_____	_____	_____
If friends or family need a babysitter or pet-minder they ask me	_____	_____	_____	_____
If I've done something wrong, I will admit it rather than try to cover up	_____	_____	_____	_____

Reliability quiz

	Always	Usually	Sometimes	Never
Even if I've made my mind up about something, I'm prepared to listen to other people's ideas and opinions	___	___	___	___
If someone makes out a convincing case, I can be persuaded to change my mind about things	___	___	___	___
I don't mind changing my plans at the last moment if there's a good reason	___	___	___	___
If I'm asked to take on work at short notice I can cope	___	___	___	___
When confronted with a problem, I like to think through several approaches before deciding how to tackle it	___	___	___	___
If I am let down by other people changing their plans, I find a way of adapting to the new circumstances	___	___	___	___
I am interested in finding out and hearing about different ideas, cultures and lifestyles	___	___	___	___
I like the idea of finding things out and learning new skills	___	___	___	___
If someone plays a practical joke upon me, I can take it in good part and share the laughter	___	___	___	___
If I make a mistake I am prepared to admit it	___	___	___	___

Looking at your experience

Given that this book is aimed at people who are looking for their first job, you probably cannot do this by describing routines and achievements in your job. It has to come across as valid experience from your hobbies, academic career, work experience and holiday/part-time jobs.

It doesn't have to be directly relevant – but the skills will be transferable. For instance, someone who is captain of a sports team is likely to be able to get on with people and to have qualities of leadership. You may disagree with this – perhaps your team captain is a despotic bully – but what you are looking for is a credible way of presenting acquired skills and experience.

If you are a loner and your hobbies are solitary, then present this as an asset: you can be left to get on with a job, you can work on your own, motivate yourself and see things through. Could you be described as a self-starter?

Someone who is involved in organising a club or group can claim experience of administration, of organising meetings and events, perhaps dealing with the press and getting publicity.

Useful phrases for self-presentation

Here are some active buzz-words which may help describe some of your achievements in a positive and up-beat way. Whatever you've done, whether it's helping as a volunteer, playing team sport or doing a holiday job, it's worth thinking about the qualities and skills you needed and the most positive way to present these to an employer, or anyone else for that matter.

Coping with routine:

conscientious	efficient
consistent	managed
controlled	performed
coped	economical
dealt with	

Working with others:

advised	managed
co-operated	negotiated
counselled	participated
facilitated	presented
guided	supervised

Achievements:

accomplished

achieved

co-ordinated

created

developed

formulated

revitalised

recommended

Problem-solving:

implemented

improved

instigated

interpreted

initiated

inspired

introduced

investigated

Initiative:

created

designed

developed

devised

directed

established

formulated

innovation

motivated

negotiated

organised

originated

solved

5

Getting an Interview

MAKING WRITTEN APPLICATIONS

There are three ways of applying for jobs in writing: letters, application forms and CVs. It's quite common to use a combination of two out of the three.

Whichever you use, there are a few written basics to get right.

Employers appreciate:
- correct spelling

- accurate punctuation

- concise, accurate summaries

- clear writing and layout

- letters accurately addressed.

Employers don't like:
- bad spelling

- poor punctuation

- rambling, vague, irrelevant information

- illegible writing and sloppy layout

- use of wrong names and/or job titles.

FILLING IN APPLICATION FORMS

Employers sometimes find it convenient to use application forms. It means that they can swiftly sort through candidates and easily make comparisons between them. Sometimes the form will have been specifically designed for the job, on other occasions it will be a general form.

Guidelines for filling in application forms

- If you know there is a job vacancy, you may have to write or ring to get a copy of the form.

- Once you've got an application form in front of you, read it through carefully before doing anything.

- It's a good idea to make a couple of photocopies of the form so that you can prepare a draft first.

- Be sure to follow the instructions – if the form tells you to use block capitals or black ink, make a point of doing just that! If an employer has a huge pile of completed forms for just one job, they often start weeding people out on the grounds that they have not followed the instructions exactly.

- Try to make sure your answers to questions fit into the space provided. If there is not enough room, you could add a separate sheet with the information on, but it is better to avoid this.

- If you feel that the form has not given you the chance to do yourself justice, you could add a copy of your CV or a covering letter. Keep it short and to the point!

- Keep a copy of the completed form and make a note of the date when you sent it to the company.

- Don't leave it until the last minute before returning the form to the company.

Application form checklist
- Follow instructions exactly.

- Make sure you write legibly.

- Fill in every section – even if only to put 'not applicable'.

- Keep a copy of what you've put on the form.

- Return the form well before the closing date.

WRITING APPLICATION LETTERS

Three golden rules
1. Think what you want to say or write.
2. Decide how to structure it – keep it logical and simple.
3. Draft the letter and check it for spelling, grammar and sense.

Guidelines for letter writing
- Be sure that your letter is legible and that it includes your name, address, contact telephone number and the date.

- Firms often advertise several vacancies at the same time, so specify which job you are applying for, and where you saw it advertised.

- Modern practice is to use plain, everyday English. Work out what you want to say, the order in which to say it and how to say it directly and clearly. Keep it simple.

- Some employers prefer to receive handwritten letters. Others find typed or word-processed material easier on the eye. Basically it's your choice. Whichever you decide on, aim for good layout and legibility.

- Try to make your letter look good. Use good quality plain paper – put a guide behind the sheet if you have trouble keeping your writing straight. Leave plenty of space around the edges of the paper, and a clear space between each paragraph.

- Write your letter out in rough, then check the spelling and punctuation. If you're not sure, use a dictionary or ask for help! When you're sure you've got it right, write your final copy.

- Write your address in the top right-hand corner.

- Write the full date below the address.

- Write the name and address of the person the letter is being sent to on the left-hand side of the letter above the Dear Sir/Madam.

- If there is a reference number, include it below the address of the person the letter is going to.

- If you know the name and title of the person you are writing to, e.g. Mr Smith, then write, 'Dear Mr Smith', and sign the letter 'Yours sincerely', followed by your name.

- If you don't know who you are writing to, then write 'Dear Sir or Madam' and end the letter with 'Yours faithfully' and your name.

- If you are writing to a woman and you don't know whether she should be addressed as Mrs or Miss, use Ms.

- Try to make the most of your experience and qualifications, but don't go too far. Calling yourself a Senior Sales Executive when you're a part-time forecourt attendant won't go down very well!

- If you've been unemployed for a spell, try and present a positive aspect of this – voluntary work or part-time study are good ways of explaining the gap!

- Print your name under your signature.

- Keep a copy of the letter.

PREPARING A CV

Some employers ask applicants to fill in an application form, while others will ask you to devise your own application.

It's usual to present the relevant information in the form of a CV – curriculum vitae. That's Latin for 'life timetable' and this piece of jargon is encountered by most jobhunters sooner or later. A CV is a summary of your personal details, education, experience and skills. In short, it's an advertisement for you.

It is common for employers to ask for a CV and application form or letter. CVs are also handy for sending 'on spec' to the personnel officers of firms you'd like to work for. Even if you don't have a computer at home, it's worth getting access to one to prepare your CV. Once the basic information is stored on disc, it makes it easier when you want to customise or tweak it for particular applications.

Preparing carefully

Writing a CV can be tricky, but it's worth spending time preparing yours. Think carefully about what you want to say about yourself, and make a few drafts before you settle on the final wording.

Format

The usual format for CVs is to use four or five basic headings to present the information.

- *Personal details*: should include full name and full address with postcode; telephone number; e-mail address; date of birth. Some people also include age, marital status, National Insurance number.

- *Education and/or qualifications and/or training*: should include information about education, training and qualifications since secondary education. Dates of attendance, and details of qualifications should be given.

- *Work experience*: list all jobs in reverse date order, i.e. starting with the most recent. Include the job title and address of the company. Where appropriate, indicate briefly what the job involved.

- *Other information*: include information about skills developed through hobbies and interests. Include things like driving licence, first aid certificate, etc.

Presenting a positive picture

It is important to present a picture of a lively individual with a lot of potential, so it is worth stressing qualifications, aspirations, hobbies and interests. Use experience gained in hobbies or community work to illustrate skills and qualities you offer an employer. Many people tend to be too modest about themselves. Be sure to include details of your most important work tasks, skills you have developed and your achievements.

Checking carefully

Take the time to make a draft (or drafts) of your CV. If you like, show it to your friends and family to check you haven't missed anything out. Check the spelling and layout, then finally get the CV typed or word-processed. Use the final version to make clear photocopies.

Checklist

- Don't make the CV too long – one page of A4 should be enough.

- Set out your personal details clearly at the top of the page.

- Give a phone number where you can be contacted during the day.

- List your exam passes clearly, showing the year you took the exams, the subjects you took and the grades you achieved.

- Give details of training programmes and work experience.

- List any awards or qualifications you gained.

- List the jobs you've had, in date order, starting with the most recent.

- Give details of part-time or voluntary work.

- List any other information you think might interest an employer, e.g. first aid training, a driving licence, languages, experience with computers or sports coaching qualification.

- Mention your hobbies and interests – especially if they're relevant to the kind of job that you want.

- Make sure the layout of your CV is clear and attractive.

SPECULATIVE APPROACHES

It may be worth writing letters to employers in case they have jobs coming up. These speculative or 'on spec' letters need to be short and to the point. They rarely lead straight to a job, but if the employer is impressed with the letter and keeps it on file, maybe next time they have a vacancy, they will invite you for an interview before going to the trouble and expense of advertising the job.

Speculative letters are a long shot. Be prepared for a low rate of return on them. However, if all you have to lose is the price of a stamp then the gamble is worth taking.

Before sending the letter, it's a good idea to try and find out the name of the person it should go to. You could try ringing the company and asking the receptionist for the name of the Department Manager or whoever is the appropriate person for you to contact.

Send a copy of your CV along with the letter.

No response

Most employers are busy people with a full workload. They don't want to spend a lot of time ploughing through irrelevant or complicated applications from people they cannot employ.

In the past it was a courtesy for employers to acknowledge applications when they had received them. Unfortunately, that is no longer the case and many employers do not contact applicants unless they have short-listed them and want to meet them. This saves the employer time and money but it adds to the uncertainty and demoralisation of the jobseeker – it's easy to imagine that all their applications are disappearing into a black hole.

If this happens to you, don't be deterred – it's nothing personal, it's just the way that organisations work. Don't take the rejection personally: some people apply for hundreds of jobs before finally succeeding. You have to believe that perseverance will be rewarded.

USING THE PHONE

Talking to people on the phone can be hard work – we hear their voice and speech but cannot see their facial expressions or body language. This means we receive much less information about the message they are giving and what they are thinking than if actually talking to them in person. So, using the phone to contact employers presents particular problems – we won't know where they are, what mood they are in and indeed whether it is a convenient time to be talking to them.

Preparing your questions

Most employers are busy people, and the chances are that they don't have time to waste. It's worth taking time to prepare. Write down a list of questions you want to ask, and if you're feeling very nervous, practise this on a friend, or household pet (at least they don't answer back). List the information you want to have found out by the time you finish the call.

Developing a good telephone manner

When you're ready, take a deep breath and keep cool. Dial the number and when someone answers, speak slowly and clearly and explain briefly why you are ringing. If you can't hear or understand what they are saying, tell them that it is a bad line and ask them to speak up and slow down. If necessary, find out the name of the person who can deal with your enquiry, and ask the person you are talking to if they can suggest a good time for you to ring back.

The aim is to be pleasant, efficient and to the point. Practise what you want to say. If you are ringing a large firm, be prepared for the fact that you may have to speak to several people before you finally get to the person you want. Keep calm, and be prepared to explain what you want as often as necessary.

One tip: smile while you're talking – the person at the other end of the phone can't see your face, but a smile actually improves the timbre of your voice.

SELECTION TESTS

Sometimes selection tests form part of the recruitment process. Here is a guide to some of the different tests used.

Aptitude tests

Some employers use aptitude tests as part of their selection procedure. These are intended to predict an individual's potential for particular types of work. An example of when aptitude tests might be used is for an assembly job in electronics, where the job requires considerable manual dexterity and hand-eye co-ordination.

Practical tests

You might be asked to do some practical tasks. This is particularly likely if you are applying for a job that requires practical skills and if you have claimed to have them e.g. demonstrating ability to use particular bits of equipment; taking dictation; demonstrating ability to use particular software packages.

Psychometric tests

These are paper and pencil tests, devised by psychologists and intended to determine aptitudes, attainments and personality. Some questions may seem rather obscure, but they don't have 'correct' answers, so there's no point in trying to second-guess them.

Graphology

Graphology is the study of handwriting. Graphologists – handwriting experts – believe that it is possible to tell a lot about people's characters from their handwriting. A few years ago there was a trend for employers to use graphology as part of their selection procedure. If you are applying for a job now, it's not particularly likely that your (handwritten) application will be subjected to scrutiny by a graphologist. However, it is possible.

If you want to find out more about graphology – perhaps to increase the chances of your handwriting and layout getting favourable interpretations – go to the library and have a look at some books on the subject. Then, forewarned, you can try and prepare the perfect script!

> 'Applications should be handwritten and accompanied by a current CV. In your letter please state why your application should receive particular consideration.'
>
> *Advertisement for trainee account manager*

Tip on tests

If you know you are going to have to do tests, try and find out what sort and get some practice. Your library may have books of tests which will help you get your hand in beforehand. However, practice doesn't really help with psychometric tests: they are intended to reveal aptitudes, attainments and personality and don't have right answers.

Work experience

Increasing numbers of students do work experience as part of their school/college courses, which can in some cases lead onto employment.

It is fairly unusual for an employer to ask a potential employee to do a spell of work experience as part of their recruitment process. However, in some industries, you may be asked to start with a temporary or part-time job.

6

Understanding Job Advertisements

AN A–Z OF EMPLOYERS' BUZZ-WORDS

Adaptable
Creative
Communicator
Confident
Drive
Enthusiastic
Flexible
Initiative

Innovative
Mobile
Motivated
Multi-tasking
Outgoing personality
Proactive
Reliable

Resilient
Resourceful
Self-starter
Smart
Task-led
Teamwork
Trustworthy

ANALYSING JOB ADVERTISEMENTS

When employers advertise posts, they usually keep the job description brief. Sometimes they send out a more detailed job specification, but if not, you must try to extract as much information as possible from the advert. Studying the wording carefully helps you avoid unnecessary stress and disappointment.

When looking at job advertisements, use this 10-point plan to analyse the post.

- The company.

- The job title and/or duties/job description.

- What does it involve – specifications for the qualifications and experience required.

- Where advertised and closing date.

- Method of application.

- Pay and other rewards.

- Hours and conditions.

- What sort of person are they looking for?

- What sort of investment are they planning to make in their employee?

- Other, e.g. travel, appearance, need for own car, etc.

Broadly speaking, job advertisements should conform to this pattern. If any information is missing, can you work out why, and does this seem reasonable? If not, it may be advisable to approach the advertisement with caution. Some areas to avoid are high pressure commission-only selling, 'opportunities' in pyramid selling (which often involve the 'employee' making a financial outlay before there is any chance of earning an income), and providing services that are of a dubious or illegal nature.

The company
A reputable company will usually give its name, address and telephone number. If the company is not identifiable, ask yourself why not? Sometimes adverts say things like 'a leading retail organisation' or 'a household name' – try and work out why they are concealing their identity. There may be a good reason, but it may be that there is something slightly suspect about the opportunity. For example, do you really want a job as a heavy breather on a soft-porn telephone service?

The job title and/or duties/job description
The advertisement should include at least an indication of what the job involves. Beware of advertisements that are vague, nebulous, over-enthusiastic or misleading.

Specifications for the qualities, qualifications and experience required
Try and work out what sort of person the employer is looking for. Does the advert specify that certain qualities are essential, desirable or preferred?

- *Essential*: if you don't have this qualification or experience you're unlikely to get to an interview.

- *Desirable*: if you don't have this qualification or experience you may get to an interview, but you will be at a disadvantage. Think about ways of presenting yourself as someone who can quickly acquire the desired skill.

- *Preferred*: the employer wants this qualification or experience, but you may still be able to talk your way into the job without it.

Method of application, where advertised and closing date
The advertisement should clearly indicate how and when to apply. If a company seems to advertise the same post(s) with monotonous regularity, draw your own conclusions.

Pay and other rewards
Not all advertisements contain this information. It obviously makes things easier for applicants if they do. Phrases like 'pay commensurate with responsibilities' and 'salary package negotiable' mean that you have to be ready to negotiate a salary at the interview stage. If this is the case, *be prepared*.

With some industries, pay grades or scales may be mentioned. If you are not familiar with these, a little research in your local library will help you come up with the current figures.

Hours and conditions
Information about the working week should be included. If no information is given, is it reasonable to assume a 35-hour Monday–Friday working week?

Are they planning to invest in the employee?
The lower the skills and qualifications specified, the lower status the job. On the other hand, a good employer is interested in retaining stall and building up their skills and experience. Making a commitment to training staff is a good sign.

Other
Statements like 'must have outgoing personality' are about the conditions of the job, not your personality. Reading between the lines, 'must have outgoing personality' means that the job involves dealing with members of the public, probably selling.

Catch phrases

What do you think the following phrases mean?

Fast-moving company

Rapidly growing company

Requires self-motivated person

Looking for a self-starter

COIGNSTONE COMMUNITY CARE
Building a future with people
Coignstone is a leading voluntary agency providing quality
supported accomodation to people with learning disabilities.
We are recruiting
FULL-TIME SUPPORT WORKERS
Salary: Res I £9,372–10,431
We are looking for the above to join experienced and
highly motivated staff teams who assist our residents to
lead valued lives within the community. These posts carry
a wide range of duties from basic care tasks to care planning.
Flexible approach and the ability to work with adults with
learning difficulties as equals required.
Previous experience in residential social work an advantage
but not essential. Sleep-ins and shift work will be required
on a rota basis.
NJC terms and conditions apply
Write for application form and information pack.
Closing date 27 February, interviews 9 March
PO Box 35, *Press & Journal*
RIBA AWARD WINNER   Investors in People Award

Looking at an example

Let's analyse the advertisement above using the 10-point plan.

The company
Coignstones Community Care . . . a voluntary organisation

Residential centre providing 'quality' care for adults with learning difficulties

Assisting them to lead valued lives within the community

The job title and/or duties/job description
Full-time support workers

The posts carry a range of duties from basic care tasks to care planning

Treating adults with learning difficulties as equals

What does it involve – specifications for the qualifications and experience required
Will require a flexible approach and the ability to work with adults with learning difficulties as equals

Residential social work experience an advantage

Working in staff teams (highly motivated staff teams)

Where advertised and closing date
Press and Journal 27th February

Method of application
Application form

Pay and other rewards
Salary: Res 1 £9,372–10,431

NJC conditions apply (NJC=National Joint Council)

Hours and conditions
Shift work and sleep-ins will be required on a rota basis
Obviously weekend work and anti-social hours

National Joint Council conditions apply

What sort of person are they looking for?
A flexible approach and the ability to work with adults with learning difficulties as equals is required

Previous experience in residential social work preferred

What sort of investment are they planning to make in their employee?
No mention, but they have 'Investors in People' award, so there is likely to be training

Also, surely training needed to offer 'quality' care

Other, e.g. travel, appearance, need for own car, etc.
Nothing else notable

Although there are gaps in the information provided, this advertisement gives you enough detail to know whether or not it is worth writing for the information pack and application form.

RESPONDING TO JOB ADVERTISEMENTS – CASE STUDIES AND EXAMPLES

Jason applies for the post of auto electrician
When employers advertise a post, they attempt to convey in a few words the sort of person they are looking for. Take the advertisement below for an auto electrician. It is very brief. It specifies that experience is required and asks for applicants to apply in writing giving details of their experience.

AUTO ELECTRICIAN
Experienced person required to install quality car audio equipment and alarm systems to a high standard.
Please apply in writing with previous experience details to
A Carling, Checkpoint, 49 George Street, Eggersley

---

62 Park Road
Eggersley Wood
EG54 7NH
Tel: 363097

A Carling
Checkpoint
49 George Street
Eggersley

September 2000

Dear Mr Carling
I am writing to apply for the post of Auto Electrician advertised in the local paper last week.

I am very interested in both cars and electronics and have fitted audio systems to cars for friends and family.

I enclose a copy of my CV.

As you will see I started doing an apprenticeship at Hudson motors but unfortunately I had to leave because I was badly hurt in a road accident. I was in hospital for six months and needed a further six months to recover. I am now fully fit and very keen to find a job.

I have recently completed a full-time course in electronics at Eggersley College. It was a very practical course involving diagnosing and repairing faults in a variety of electronic kit.

I realise that you are probably looking for someone with more experience than me, but I am extremely keen to learn and would be happy to demonstrate my skills to you.

The service manager at Hudsons and my electronics tutor at college will be happy to give me references.
I do hope you will consider my application.

Yours sincerely

Jason Parker

Fig. 1. Jason's letter of application.

CURRICULUM VITAE

Name: Jason Parker
Address: 62 Park Road, Eggersley Wood
Date of birth: 29.3.80
Telephone   363097

Education Qualifications
Eggersley FE College   NVQ level 2 Diploma in
1999   Electronics

Stoke Hatton FE College Studied vehicle mechanics
Day release 1996–8

Lawton Wood School   GCSE
1991–1996   Maths (C), English (D),
                         Technology (C), Physics (C),
                         Music (C)

Work Experience
Hudson Motors Ltd   Apprentice car mechanic
1996–8

Other Experience
I have a full clean driving licence and my own transport.
I have fitted audio and alarm systems to cars for my friends
and family.
I have a first aid certificate.

Interests
I manage a rock band and set up and sort out their sound
system at gigs and recording sessions.
I am captain of the Black Bull quiz team.
I was secretary of the college social committee which
involved setting up entertainers, booking bands, arranging
publicity and generally making sure things ran smoothly.

Fig. 2. Jason's CV.

From the information provided by the advertisement the main criterion is experience fitting audio and alarm systems – 'quality' systems installed to a 'high standard'. There is no mention of training. If you were keen on this job and had gained some experience of fitting systems as a hobby, there would be nothing to lose by applying, but it would be a long shot.

Now look at Jason's application letter and CV in Figures 1 and 2.

Coral applies for the receptionist job

This advertisement, for a Receptionist/Office Junior, makes no mention of experience. Describing the job as Office Junior implies that experience is not expected. No mention is made of qualifications either but appearance and manner are emphasised. This is one of the instances when a handwritten letter is required.

Coral O'Rourke is applying for the job. She has adopted a very upbeat attitude to presenting herself (see Figures 3 and 4). Do you think her approach is a good one? Would you give her an interview and what do you think are her chances of getting the job?

ROBSON'S FINANCIAL SERVICES
require a
Receptionist/Office Junior
for their busy city centre office
The successful applicant will be sales-orientated, have a
smart appearance and pleasant confident manner when
answering the telephone or dealing with clients in person
Apply in own handwriting with brief CV

'Horses for courses'

Compare the two contrasting advertisements on page 87 for someone to do DTP (Desk Top Publishing). Although both advertisements are aimed at people with DTP skills, they take very different forms and very different sorts of responses are appropriate.

Chris Callendar has prepared a fairly traditional application for the first job (see Figure 5). The letter is low key and does not make a big impact. The question is whether it will make enough of an impression to get Chris invited for an interview.

Coral O'Rourke
14 Nettleby House, Nettleby Road, Cotham DC3 6YH
Tel: 934176

The Manager
Robson's Financial Services

14 October

Dear Sir or Madam

I am writing to apply for the job of Receptionist/Office Junior advertised in the local paper.

I am 18 years old and have just left college where I have been studying Business. I am hoping to make my career in financial services and particularly enjoy selling.

Throughout my course I worked one day a week at Scott Insurance Brokers in Main Street. My role included a variety of jobs involving working in the reception area and in the back office. I used computers to prepare quotes for customers, did filing and carried out general office work.

For the last three years I have worked as a Saturday sales assistant at Indigo Boutique. I am outward going and enjoy selling quality goods to the public. We work on a commission basis, and I have consistently been the top Saturday sales assistant.

I enclose my CV and am available for interview at any time in the next two weeks. Lorna Irons, the Manager at Indigo and Peter Stephenson at Scott's will both give me glowing references.

I look forward to meeting you.

Yours sincerely

Coral O'Rourke

Fig. 3. Coral's application letter.

CURRICULUM VITAE

Coral O'Rourke
14 Nettleby House, Nettleby Road, Cotham DC3 6YH
Tel: 934176

Profile
I am a smart, self-confident, self-starter looking for a
suitable role in financial sales.

I enjoy dealing with the public and am ambitious and
outgoing.

I am confident using word processing, spreadsheet and
presentation packages on computers.

Education	*Qualifications*
Cotham 6th Form College 1998–9	GNVQ Business
Cotham Secondary School 1991–1998	GCSE English (D), Maths (C), Art (C),

Work experience	*Duties*
Scott Insurance Brokers 1998–9	Work experience trainee
Indigo Boutique 1996–present	Part time sales assistant

Other experience
Two years ago I set up a club to arrange tickets and
transport for events outside the area. To date I have
organised trips to concerts and gigs. I am currently
organising tickets and transport for 30 people from the
college to go to the Fashion Show next month.

Interests and hobbies
Fashion, music, organising things.

Fig. 4. Coral's CV.

Keen hard-working junior with creative
and keyboard skills required to train in DTP
Apply in writing to Gil Gray,
Danata, The Studio, West Walls,
Dacre Mount

Graphic Artist
WE'RE LOOKING FOR TWO RISING STARS
Aberdour Publishers seeks two bright young creatives
with shining portfolios, looking for a bright future.
If you are enthusiastic, ambitious and have a desire for
clarity in the business of communication, then we are
interested.
The successful applicants must demonstrate strong
visual and design skills using the Apple Macintosh
and proficiency using Freehand, Quark Express and
Photoshop.
Previous advertising experience will be an advantage.
Please send a communication that expresses creatively
your talents and ambitions to
Studio Manager, Aberdour Publishing

The second job clearly requires a rather different response. It is advertising for a creative and imaginative person with well-developed visual realisation skills. This advertisement invites anyone interested to 'send a communication' expressing their creative talents.

What sort of reply are they asking for? A letter, a video, a computer-generated graphic? This is one of those opportunities (rare in the field of job applications) to indulge creative talents and prepare something very distinctive. The employers want applicants to make an impression. If you've got the imagination and the skills, then let rip!

Gil Gray
Danata, The Studio
West Walls, Dacre Mount

30 May

Dear Gil Gray

I am writing to apply for the job of DTP trainee advertised in the local paper.

I am 20 years old and have just completed a GNVQ in Art & Design.

I did an Advanced GNVQ – a two-year full-time course equivalent to 2 A levels. I have always wanted to be a graphic artist and I chose the course because it is a practical, work related qualification offering the skills, knowledge and understanding for a broad range of jobs in Art & Design.

In my course I did Art & Design units, core skills units to develop skills in communication, information technology and working with numbers, and I specialised in computer graphics. I have used a variety of software including Photoshop, Freehand Quark Express and PageMaker.

I did a work placement at The MacTavish Studio in Main Street.

I enclose my CV and hope that you will consider my application. I would be happy to bring my portfolio in to show you the standard of work I achieved. My college tutor, Irene Bell and Fergus McTavish from McTavish Studio have both agreed to act as referees.

I look forward to hearing from you.

Yours sincerely

Chris Callendar

Fig. 5. Chris Callendar's conventional application.

7

Finding the Openings

It's fine knowing how to prepare an impeccable CV and application letter but in order to apply these skills, you have to track down some vacancies to apply for!

USING SPECIALISTS

Jobcentres

Jobcentres are easy to use (and they don't cost anything) – just walk in and look at the card displays showing job vacancies locally and in other parts of the country. If you find a suitable vacancy, one of the staff will phone the employer to arrange an interview for you. Jobcentres get details of around 30 per cent of all job vacancies.

Careers offices

Careers Companies keep details of local vacancies for younger people, including training places. Careers Officers have specialist knowledge about all sorts of jobs, as well as knowing the local job market.

Employment agencies

Commercial employment agencies operate in large towns and cities. Their business is to find staff to fill job vacancies notified by employers. They usually make their money by charging the employer, not the jobseeker. Be extremely wary of any agency that tries to get you to pay them: registration fees, placement fees, whatever they call them – forget it. In most cases it's against the law (exceptions include the entertainment business and fashion modelling).

Some agencies specialise in placing people in particular job fields, e.g. cleaning work, secretarial work, computer work or machine work. If they find you a job, you will be an employee of that company and paid by them. In addition, they will pay the agency a fee or percentage for finding you.

Many agencies will only take on to their books people with specific work skills and, preferably, experience. Other agencies are contracted by employers to provide man/woman-power and complete set work tasks. Typically a factory may be meeting a sudden order and need extra staff in the packing department. The company will contract an agency to provide temporary staff for the duration of the rush. In this case, you would be employed by the agency, not the factory. Once that job finishes the agency might move you on to another job.

If you are planning to use an agency, the Federation of Recruitment and Employment Services, 36–38 Mortimer Street, London W1N 7RB produces a factsheet on selecting agencies. Send SAE for a copy.

Why do employers use agencies?
• To save advertising.

• To save the administration and hassle of employing people.

• To avoid being swamped with job applicants.

• To cut down the work of the Personnel Department.

On-line agencies
The Internet is hosting a boom in on-line recruitment agencies. Initially a source of IT jobs it's now starting to catch on in other sectors. The more sophisticated sites invite you to register what you are looking for – job title, location, salary, and will notify you by e-mail of any appropriate vacancies. See page 118 for some current URLs.

Joining a jobclub
If you've been out of work and signing on for a while you might be asked to join a local Jobclub. The Jobclub objective is 'to help you get the best possible job in the shortest time'. They do this by providing advice and guidance on job-hunting techniques and by providing free facilities – photocopying, phones, desks and postage. In return, Jobclub members usually agree to attend for four half-day sessions each week and to pursue up to ten job leads every day. The Jobclub philosophy is that there are jobs for

people who want them, and that if you haven't got one it's because you haven't yet uncovered sufficient vacancies, or because you have not presented yourself in the best light.

Joining a Jobclub may help you maintain morale; it will bring you into contact with others in a similar situation and will ensure that you use a systematic, structured approach to job hunting.

SPOTTING ADVERTISEMENTS

Depending on the job, you may find appropriate advertisements in newspapers, magazines and trade papers.

Reading local newspapers

Local papers carry a range of advertisements for skilled and unskilled people. If it is a weekly paper, then jobs will be advertised every week. If it is a daily or evening paper, there may be particular days when job advertisements are featured.

Reading national newspapers

Some of the national newspapers carry job advertisements. To be in the running for these jobs you are likely to need qualifications and skills.

Each of the broadsheets feature advertisements for particular types of jobs. If you think you may be able to find a career in this way, go to the library and study the target audience for the different papers. Be sure to carry out your survey over a full week as there may be a pattern to the advertising.

For example, *The Telegraph* is good if you want to get into production, sales or engineering. *The Guardian* features different types of jobs each day. At present there are as follows:

Monday	Creative, media, PR, marketing, sales and secretarial
Tuesday	Education
Wednesday	Public service (health, housing, social care and environment) and volunteers
Thursday	Computers, IT, science and technology
Saturday	All the week's advertisements and graduate section (aimed at new graduates)

Checking the trade papers

Some occupations and trades have their own publications: papers, magazines and bulletins. If you have skills and qualifications in a particular line then it may be worth subscribing to your own journal or checking it regularly in the library.

Every career has its own specialist publications. If you've recently trained in a particular line of work but are not sure where jobs are advertised, ask one of your tutors to advise you. If your local library does not have a subscription to your trade journal, it's always worth suggesting to them that they take one out.

The Internet

For the computer-literate, cyberspace offers up-to-the minute information about job skills and vacancies. Many companies include current job vacancies on their web sites. Use a search engine to find companies that interest you and then study their employment sections. Some sites include facilities to compile and or submit CVs on-line. See page 118 for list of URLs for jobseekers.

OTHER APPROACHES

Working the grapevine

Research suggests that as many as 50 per cent of job vacancies are never advertised. To be in the market for these 'hidden vacancies', put out the word among your family and friends and ask them to let you know of any possibilities they hear of.

Creating opportunities

Think laterally about ways of making yourself known to employers. For the out-going personality, possibilities might include advertising yourself; creating a publicity stunt to gain local newspaper or radio coverage; making a video or audio cassette advertising your skills.

Cold calling

'Cold calling' or 'cold canvassing' means making an unsolicited approach to someone to try and sell them something. For the job hunters, cold calling means visiting or telephoning companies and trying to sell yourself to them!

In some books about finding work (particularly by American

authors) cold calling is strongly advocated as part of the drive to find work. However, whether in person or on the telephone, cold calling takes a lot of confidence, persistence and bravado. Not everyone has the personality and resilience to cope with it.

The first step is to find the name of the person with the power to hire and fire, and then to get access to them. If you decide to give it a go, it's important to prepare yourself and practise what you want to say. You need to be pleasant, persistent and succinct.

Think about what you want to say and try writing a short 'advertisement for yourself'. Get a trusted friend to help you practise. Ask them to play the role of the Personnel Officer or Manager. Run through the scenario several times, with your friend taking on different personalities.

See the section on interview questions in Chapter 8.

LOOKING FURTHER AFIELD

Daily travel possibilities

Creative approaches to solving problems means thinking laterally. If there are no jobs to be had in your immediate travel-to-work area, what about looking further afield?

Start off by considering your daily travelling distance, where you can reasonably go to work for the day. Make a map with your house at the centre. Mark in travel-to-work times in different directions using all feasible means of transport. If necessary, investigate trains, buses and any other public transport, cycle, car, motor bike or lifts.

Moving on?

For some people, 'getting on their bike' and moving to find work is not a serious possibility. However, if you are young and fancy free, it may be worth considering. Living in another part of the country, or indeed abroad, can be a great experience. If you are unemployed and undecided you could look for seasonal work in a holiday resort – lots of jobs in hotels and holiday camps come with accommodation provided. It's probably not what you want to spend your life doing, but as short-term experience it can have a lot to recommend it (not least, a wild social life).

STICKING AT IT

You can't expect to stumble across the perfect job the day you start searching. Don't expect overnight success – finding a job can take time and effort. Dig in, plan your campaign methodically, and above all follow it through. The jobhunters most likely to succeed behave as though they are already working, getting up in the morning, and spending hours each day scanning the papers, visiting the Jobcentre, writing letters, making phone calls and following up leads for as long as it takes. It helps to keep a log of your applications, as in the example in Figure 6.

Organisation	Contact name and number	Date and how contacted	Response	Action
ULC	Human Resources Department (!!) Tel: ext 4659	Letter, 20 June	Holding letter received 5 July	Me to write again in September
CT Rawlinsons Ltd	Olivia O'Neil, PA to Managing Director, Operations Tel: 332178	I phoned 30 June for application form	Application form to complete	Check OK with referees. Wait for interview?
Foresters	Malcom Singer 456773	Rang 3 June	Told me to call in for application form	Application form and CV sent in. Wait to hear . . .
The Spotted Dog ice cream parlour needs relief staff during the summer months	Linda George Manager 356 73245	Went in 28 June for a coffee and got chatting, hence found out about possibilities . . .	OK – they'll ring me if they need extra staff at weekend	Make sure I'm in at 6.00 p.m. on Fridays in case they ring

Fig. 6. Job applications log.

JOBSEEKER'S CHECKLIST

Preparing for jobhunting

- Are you clear about what work you are looking for?

- Have you prepared a CV recently?

- Does your CV do you justice?

- Are you getting support and encouragement – from friends, family, Jobclub, etc. – in your jobhunt?

Careers Office or Jobcentre

- When did you last visit the Careers Office or Jobcentre?

- Are you planning another visit?

Employment agencies

- Have you checked out employment agencies in your area?

- Are you keeping in contact with them?

Papers and magazines

- Do you check every edition of your local paper(s) for jobs?

- Do you look in national papers for jobs?

- Do you look in trade journals for jobs?

The Internet

- When did you last use the Internet to look for work?

- Have you tried different search engines with queries for local employers and agencies?

Speculative approaches

- Do you write speculative letters to possible employers?

- Do you make speculative phone calls to possible employers?

- Have you tried making speculative visits to companies?

The grapevine

- Do your friends and family all know you are looking for work?

- Do you watch out for new developments locally?

Interviews

- Are you happy with your interview technique?

8

Shining at an Interview

Congratulations, you've cleared the first set of obstacles and you've been invited to an interview. Well done, but there's still work to be done. Before you go for the interview you need to prepare yourself.

DOING YOUR HOMEWORK

Swotting up on the company

Set yourself the task of discovering as much as you can about the company/organisation. Remember, you're trying to convince the person interviewing you that you want to work in their organisation. It will improve your chances if you show that you have taken an interest in the company and have some idea about their business.

Try and find out as much information as possible. Here are some ideas about the sorts of details you might be able to discover:

- What is the business of the company, i.e. what do they do/make?

- How many people do they employ?

- How many branches/factories/offices do they have and where are they situated?

- When did the company start?

- Where will I be working?

- What will I be paid?

- What are the arrangements for holidays?

- What is the public transport like?

- Is there somewhere to park?

- What hours will I work?

- When is the lunch break?

- Are there canteen facilities?

- Is there overtime?

- Is there extra pay for working overtime?

- Why does the vacancy exist?

- What are the promotion prospects?

Sources of information

Some employers send out an information pack with the job specification and application forms. Others will send information with the interview invitation. It's a good idea to be very thorough in reading through whatever documentation the employer provides. Not only does this give you background information about the company and its operations, but if you reach the interview and you haven't read the information they have given you it gives the impression that you are not interested in the job and don't have the motivation to sit down and do basic homework.

Other possible sources of information about a company include:

- any employees you know

- company annual report

- company newsletter or website

- company publicity material.

Swotting up on interview techniques

Many employers have no training in interviewing people, and the person who is going to interview you may be nearly as nervous as you are! It's important to get a grip on the situation, act confidently and make sure you present yourself as well as possible.

Be prepared – perhaps you could ask one of your friends or family to have a practice run through with you. Get them to take the role of the interviewer and ask the questions they think you will be asked. If you have access to a video camera, perhaps you could record a 'mock interview'. This can be a good way of learning how you can improve your interview technique.

MAKING AN IMPRESSION

It has been established that most people form 90 per cent of their opinion of someone within a minute and a half of meeting them! Subsequent meetings and conversations may make them change their mind, but it could be an uphill struggle to get them to rectify first impressions that are wrong. It's worth thinking about this because the first moments of your interview are vital! As first impressions count for such a lot, it's really important to be positive and well prepared.

Preparing for an interview means more than thinking about how to answer questions: it means giving some thought to how you come across – appearance, attitude and mannerisms. Consider carefully what your appearance will say about you in those vital few moments. When you've got the place to yourself, put on your interview outfit and look at yourself in a full-length mirror. Try and see what sort of image you give. Seek a second opinion from friends or family whose judgement you respect.

See the section on appearance in Chapter 3.

Non-verbal communication

Whenever we meet someone, especially someone new, we form an impression of them before they have even opened their mouths and spoken one word. People convey a whole range of messages about themselves by their appearance, attitude and mannerisms. This means that interviews aren't just about what you say, they are about the way you come across. The popular term given to this is 'body language'.

Animals rely entirely on non-verbal communication. Some of their signals are very familiar to us. Bared teeth signify aggression; the wagging tail of a dog is a gesture of friendship; a bull pawing the ground means trouble and so on.

With humans, being able to talk doesn't stop us using non-verbal signals. In face-to-face meetings, words actually contribute less than one-third of the message. The other two-thirds is non-verbal: gestures, head movements, posture, body position, facial expression, eye contact, proximity and touch. Body language tends to convey emotions and attitudes. It plays an important part when people meet face to face, especially for the first time.

Any interaction between people involves communicating in different ways at different levels. A lot of this happens without us realising it. Words are used mainly for conveying information, while the non-verbal channel (body language) tends to give information about people's character and personality; their emotions and attitudes. So in any face-to-face dealings with people, we are giving out a lot of unspoken messages. People we come into contact with invariably use these signals in forming their impressions and ideas about us. In preparing for interviews, it's worth giving some time and thought to making sure that the messages that get across are the ones we want to give!

Learning about body language

Even if we cannot hear what people are saying, it's often possible to understand some of their communication from watching facial expressions, gestures and other body language. Watch the TV with the sound down, or look at photos of people and try and work out from their postures and expressions what they are feeling. How much can you tell about the relationships between people?

Strong emotions like anger, love, fear are readily communicated by body language. How far can the qualities employers look for, like self-confidence, honesty, intelligence, adaptability, drive, resilience, determination, patience, originality, responsibility, resourcefulness, etc., be conveyed by body language?

Studies of human communication suggest that the average person speaks words for only a total of 10 or 11 minutes in the whole day and that the average sentence takes only about two and a half seconds. Surprising, isn't it? If you don't believe it, why not get out your stopwatch and check!

UNDERSTANDING INTERVIEW FORMATS

The standard interview format is for one or two people from the employing organisation to interview a candidate. Be prepared: not all organisations do things the same way. There are variations such as:

- panel interview

- aptitude tests

- group interview

- group initiative exercises

- familiarisation

- work experience.

> 'I was surprised and flattered to be shortlisted for a new job with a voluntary organisation. When I went into the interview room, I was flabbergasted to find myself facing a panel of 13: it seemed that all the committee were to be involved in the selection process.
>
> It was a nightmare. The Chairman started off introducing them all by name but by the time we got to number 13, I couldn't remember any of them! As the interview progressed it became clear that each person had their own agenda for me to address. I found it extremely difficult: I didn't know who to look at, which person to address my answers to. I knew I should be making eye contact but how do you do that with 13 people?
>
> I didn't get the job, and I don't envy the person who did!'
>
> *Applicant for job with community organisation*

Pattern of interviews

Every interview is unique which makes it impossible to predict what will happen. However, in general terms, an interview is likely to follow the pattern described below. Depending on the company and the job, some of these elements may be left out and others may be extended.

Before the interview starts
1. Candidate(s) arrive.
2. May be introduced to various members of staff.
3. May be shown around the company/organisation.

Once the interview starts
1. Candidate enters room.
2. Introduction.
3. Opening pleasantries.
4. Information given.
5. Checking facts.
6. Assessing abilities.
7. Assessing personality.
8. Assessing motivation.
9. Candidate asks questions.
10. Candidate is told when and how they will hear the outcome of the interview.
11. Interview finishes and candidate leaves the room.

An example of an interviewer's brief

Below is a copy of a brief used by one interviewer. It uses a six-point plan as a framework for the interview, and lists various skills and qualities that the interviewer should try and establish during the meeting.

1. *Physical*
Body build, health, strength, eyesight, any disabilities.

2. *Skills and abilities*
Hobbies
Favourite subject
Manual or craft skills
Artistic ability

3. *Interests*
Spare time activities
Reading habits
Interests in social or political issues
Questions to ask:
What do you do in your spare time?
How much time do you spend on an activity?

What are you reading now/What was the last book you read?
What sort of music do you like? Who is your favourite band?
  Why?

4. *Personality*
Confidence
Attitude to people
Warmth
Humour
Anxiety
Questions to ask:
How do you get on with other people?
Are you good at . . . ?
Describe your strengths and weaknesses.

5. *Circumstances*
Living at home or not
Financial position
Commitments to people or places or activities

6. *Achievements*
Qualifications
Certificates
Badges
Records of achievement
Exam results

The interviewer
It's impossible to give foolproof and detailed guidelines about
what to say in an interview situation! However well you prepare,
there is still the element of luck in it. Employers want people with
enthusiasm, ability, the right skills and attitudes as well as the
potential for development. Different interviewers in different
situations look for, and are impresssed by, different qualities. The
interview is where they try and spot who has what they are
looking for. A tall order as some interviews are as short as 15
minutes.
   We all carry around with us assumptions, stereotypes and
prejudices. Interviewers, however well trained, are no different
which means that there may be times when there are inherent
inadequacies in the interview process.
   Take, as an example, an employer who is advertising for a

personal assistant. Owing to an unfortunate childhood experience, this person has a particular aversion to West Midlands accents. Now there's absolutely nothing wrong with this – or any other – regional accent, but in this instance if your accent shrieks Brum, then it's likely that, however well-qualified you are, it's unlikely you will get beyond the interview stage. It's very unfortunate, but an interview with you is not going to change this interviewer's attitude. It's hard to give constructive advice about coping with this sort of situation. Basically you have to accept it, without letting it demoralise you, and move on to the next opportunity, where hopefully they will appreciate your accent.

First impressions

Nerve-wracking though it is, your interview effectively starts when you enter the company's premises. Even if you have to spend time sitting in the reception area waiting to be called by the interviewers, you are on show and it's a good idea to act accordingly. The receptionist who points you to a chair may not be the Managing Director of the company, but you never know . . . maybe the Personnel Officer will ask him/her for impressions of the people who have been called in for an interview. So try and be friendly and polite and use an ashtray, not the floor, if you smoke.

INTERVIEW QUESTIONS

Employers sometimes throw difficult questions into interviews – sometimes intentionally to see how you will cope; sometimes without meaning to, because they are not very good at interviewing. If this happens, keep calm and don't panic: as long as you are prepared you will be able to cope.

Coping with difficult questions

An excellent way of learning strategies and techniques for coping with awkward questions – questions you don't know the answer to or questions you don't want to answer – is to watch politicians being interviewed on TV.

If you don't understand the question, ask for clarification. Don't be embarrassed to ask the interviewer to repeat the question. If you need to play for time take a leaf out of the politicians' book: 'That's a very interesting question. I'm glad you asked me that.'

Here are some difficult questions interviewers might use to put you on the spot. It's worth preparing your answers beforehand. The technique for dealing with very open-ended questions like 'tell me about yourself' is to have prepared short, positive and concise answers which relate to the post you have applied for. Try to avoid dwelling on the personal and concentrate on the work-related aspect of questions.

- Tell me about yourself.

- What do you see yourself doing in ten years time?

- How well do you get on with other people?

- Why do you want this job?

- What qualities would you bring to the job?

- Why should we employ you?

- Why do you want to work here?

- How much pay are you looking for?

- How do you cope with pressure?

- What are your strengths?

- What are your weaknesses?

- What is the most difficult situation you have faced?

- What are the two most important things that have happened in the last five years?

- What kind of experience do you have for this job?

- Why do you think you can do this job?

INTERVIEW SCRIPTS

The nightmare interview: interview for a post of Retail Assistant in a DIY superstore

Interviewer Tell me about yourself.

Applicant Er well, you've got my application form, it's all there (*awkward pause*). Um, what sort of thing do you want to know?

Interviewer For example, how do you get on with other people?

Applicant Fine.

Interviewer Well, perhaps you can tell me why you want this job?

Applicant Um, well, it's really near my house and the pay seems quite good, so I thought I'd apply.

Interviewer That's very good of you. What do you know about the company?

Applicant Er, well, I've been in the shop a couple of times.

Interviewer Why do you think you can do this job?

Applicant Well, I don't see why I can't.

Interviewer What qualities would you bring to the job?

Applicant Um, what do you mean?

Interviewer You've applied for a job as a Retail Assistant. As you probably realise, this means working with the general public, dealing with enquiries and ensuring customer satisfaction. Why would you be an asset to the company? What qualities would you bring to the job?

Applicant Oh, right, I see what you mean. Well, I'd be OK, I mean I'm not stupid. I get on all right.

Interviewer Well, thank you for taking the time to come along. We have several other candidates to interview and will be in touch when we have decided.

Let's face it, that did not go at all well. How could our applicant have done better with a bit of preparation and planning?

The re-run: interview for a post of Retail Assistant in a DIY superstore

Interviewer Tell me about yourself.

Applicant I'm very practical and I enjoy solving problems. As you can see from my application form, I left school a few months ago and while I've been looking for work, I've been doing a lot of jobs at home. I redecorated my room and at the moment I'm doing some tiling in the bathroom.

Interviewer Are you working on your own?

Applicant You wouldn't ask that if you saw the size of our bathroom – it's microscopic!

Interviewer I see. How well do you get on with other people?

Applicant Oh very well. I enjoy being part of a team. I play in a mixed hockey team in the leagues at the leisure centre.

Interviewer Why do you want this job?

Applicant Well, as I said, I've been doing a lot of DIY at home and I've been coming into the store quite a bit. I quite often ask the assistants for advice about the things you sell and it seems a very interesting job. I think I'd enjoy the contact with customers and also I'm interested in the products you sell.

Interviewer Why do you think you can do this job?

Applicant I'm physically fit and I can operate a till and do credit card transactions. I did that when I worked in a supermarket last summer.

Interviewer What qualities would you bring to the job?

Applicant   Um, what do you mean?

Interviewer You've applied for a job as a Retail Assistant. As you probably realise, this means working with the general public, dealing with enquiries and ensuring customer satisfaction. Why would you be an asset to the company? What qualities would you bring to the job?

Applicant Oh, right, I see what you mean. Well I'd be OK. I can talk to people and I'm interested in DIY and home improvements. I know there's a lot more to learn, but I am keen.

Interviewer   Well, thank you for taking the time to come along. We have several other candidates to interview and will be in touch when we have decided.

Another nightmare scenario: the hopeless interviewer

However well prepared you may be, some interviews do not go according to plan . . .

Interviewer Good afternoon, I'm the Duty Manager for Lathoms. You are . . . ?

Applicant   Nicky Jarvis. I'm here for an interview.

Interviewer Oh yes, right. Let me just find your details. Well, while I'm finding them perhaps you can tell me a bit about yourself.

Applicant   Right, well I've just completed a GNVQ in Leisure and Tourism at college and I'm now looking for a full-time job. As you can see, I've had various part-time jobs and work placements in the leisure industry and I'm very keen on all sorts of sport and I enjoy working with people . . .

Interviewer So why do you want this job?

Applicant   Well, according to the advert, the post of Leisure Assistant is a good opportunity to broaden my experience.

Interviewer Oh, sorry, I thought you were here for the job in the kitchen.

Applicant I'm happy to help out with catering in an emergency, but I understood the main duties were in the Leisure Centre itself.

Interviewer Right, here we are, I've found your application form. Now let's see . . . what are you offering us?

Applicant I've got the silver life-saving medal and . . .

Interviewer Well, we don't have a swimming pool, so that won't be much use.

Applicant I've got certificates in basic first aid and instructing aerobics.

Interviewer We don't do aerobics.

Applicant Maybe I could start a class for you, it's very popular . . .

WHAT DO YOU ASK?

The questions most candidates have at the top of their list relate to pay and conditions – hours of work, holidays, overtime, etc. However, when invited to ask questions, it doesn't create the right impression to leap straight in with the selfish considerations. You will want this information, but it's worth writing down in advance a few questions relating to other issues which might not be covered during the interview.

Questions you might want to ask include:

- What sort of training might I get?

- Would the company support me if I wanted to get further training?

- If appointed, who would I report to?

- What is the line management?

- How do you do staff appraisals?

- What are the areas of company growth?

- What are the promotion opportunities?

- Does the company promote from within?

- In what ways is the organisation likely to change in the next couple of years?

FEEDBACK AND REVIEWING

If you don't succeed in getting the job, it's tempting to put it all behind you and move on to the next opportunity. However, whether or not you get the job, there are still things you can learn from the encounter. As they say, experience is the name we give to our mistakes, but in order to learn from it we need to review what happened and identify any lessons it has to offer.

After an interview, you may feel that thinking about it is the last thing you want to do with your time. However, it is worth making the effort to look back at it and review what happened. Even if you didn't succeed in getting that job, learning from the experience may stand you in good stead next time. Remember, the point of reviewing is to look back at what happened and work out what went well and what went badly in order to plan how to handle the situation better next time.

Making notes

A good strategy is to try and make notes about the interview when it is over. Write down anything you can remember: for example, what questions were asked and how you responded. It could be worth making separate lists of the things you coped with well, and the questions and or situation that caused problems (see the example in Figure 7). It is a good idea to make a note of the names and job titles of the people you met while you were being interviewed and shown around.

Questions they asked	Answers I gave	How I felt about the way I handled it
'Why do you want to work for us?'	'The company has a very good reputation and I think the opportunities for training are better in a large company	Like a creep but it seemed to go down OK with them!
'You say you are keen on getting training. Which areas of our operation particularly interest you?'	'Well, that is a good question, but I don't really know enough about the company to rule anything out. I imagine that after a few months familiarisation I'll have more idea.'	Whoops, caught me out! Didn't know enough detail, had to waffle. Felt very hot under the collar. Hope they didn't spot it.
'You say on your application form that in your work experience at Dobbinsons you did general office administration. Can you tell me more about that, please?'	'Well, I was in the finance department for two weeks and they didn't really give me anything interesting to do. I made a lot of coffee and took the post out. It was a bit disappointing, because I think they could have given me more interesting things to do, more responsibility.'	I should have been more positive . . . Maybe said: 'I would have enjoyed a longer placement as I wasn't there long enough to get my teeth into things, but it gave me the flavour of the work of the office and made me appreciate the administration side of business.'
'How did you get on with the staff there?'	Er, all right . . . they were all OK but unfortunately, no one really took responsibility for helping me get settled in.'	I felt as though this interview was on the wrong tack . . . needed to change its direction to something more positive.
'You've also worked at Supersavers during your holidays. How did you get on with the supervisors there?'	'Oh, very well, I found them extremely good to work for. They always gave very clear instructions and if there was a problem I knew who to refer it to.'	Phew, that's a bit more like it.

What went well?
Talking about computers, my qualifications and experience at Supersavers.

What went badly?
I was fine with the specific questions, but when they invited me to talk about myself I tended to waffle on a bit and be too modest and self-effacing. Not a good move to moan about Dobbinson's old ratbag who ruined my work experience.

How could I handle the situation better next time?
Don't mention negative things or personality clashes – it gives the wrong impression. Concentrate on positive aspects of the experience, e.g. became expert at coping with a temperamental office photocopier.

Fig. 7. Example interview review sheet.

Listening to feedback

Some personnel officers give all candidates some feedback about how they came across. Even if you don't get the job, it's worth listening to this because it can help you do better next time.

Sometimes the results of interviews are announced at the time. Otherwise, applicants are told they will hear one way or the other, usually by post, but sometimes by telephone. If there is a chance that you will get a call from them, it's a good idea to make sure you have a note of the names and job titles of the people that you met. It may be a good idea to keep it by your phone so that, if one of them rings you to ask further questions (or to offer you the job), you will be well prepared to talk to them.

Even if the organisation uses a short, standard letter to reject you, you can still seek feedback. If you're feeling particularly positive, you could write to or ring the personnel office or interviewer, and ask them for some feedback. If you do this, make clear to them that you're asking in order to improve your performance next time, rather than asking them to justify their decision.

Appendix 1
Form Filling

If you're looking for your first job, it's worth making a Personal Databank of the information you may be asked. Use a card index, loose-leaf file or simple computer system to collect and record names, addresses, telephone numbers and dates you may need.

Here is a compilation of questions taken from a selection of application forms. It is unlikely that one employer would ask all these questions, but if you are applying for a number of jobs you could be asked for a lot of this information.

- Full name

- Address

- Telephone number

- Fax number and/or e-mail address

- Date of birth

- Age

- Marital status

- NI number

- Nationality

- Passport number

- Place of birth

- Position applied for

- Education, secondary schools/colleges attended, with dates

- Further/higher education, with examinations taken and dates

- Other training courses

- Qualifications and dates taken

- Work experience with dates

- Job title and description of duties

- Are you prepared to relocate?

- Hobbies

- Interests

- Salary received

- Have you ever applied to this company before?

- Referees (give names of two or three professional people who can vouch for your work)

- Have you been convicted of any criminal offence, including offences which are not yet 'spent' under the Rehabilitation of Offenders Act 1979?

- Do you have a full clean driving licence?

- Medical history – list any illnesses you have suffered

- Do you have a First Aid qualification?

- Are you a registered disabled person?

- What salary do you expect?

- Name and address of next of kin

- If appointed, when would you be available to start?

- How did you hear about this vacancy?

- Parents' nationalities, places and dates of birth (the Civil Service ask for this information).

Appendix 2
National Vocational Qualifications

National Vocational Qualifications or NVQs (SVQs, Scottish Vocational Qualifications, in Scotland) are awarded for what people know and can do. If you can show that you have the appropriate skills and knowledge, you can get an NVQ. Each NVQ is made up of a number of units which set out the standards required in a range of tasks. If you can show that you meet the standard for a unit you are awarded a credit for it. Demonstrating this competence may take the form of projects, coursework, discussion or a demonstration at work.

The NVQ is awarded once all the units have been achieved. However, as there is no time limit or set order in which the units have to be done, NVQs are very flexible and can be acquired at a pace which suits each individual.

National Record of Achievement
People working towards NVQs often keep a National Record of Achievement (NRA). This is a sort of log book containing information about achievements and experience in education, training, employment and in life. It provides a positive record of the owner's training and development. An NRA can help at interviews for training or employment.

GNVQs
General National Vocational Qualifications (GNVQs) (GSVQs in Scotland) are for young people who want to gain practical, work-related qualifications. There are eight occupational areas available at three levels:

- Foundation GNVQ – usually a one-year full-time course equivalent to 4 GCSEs at grade D or below.

- Intermediate GNVQ – usually a one-year full-time course equivalent to 4 GCSEs at grades A to C.

- Advanced GNVQ – usually a two-year full-time course equivalent to 2 GCE A levels.

GNVQs help students develop skills, knowledge and understanding which are a grounding for a broad range of jobs. Students' courses can be tailored to meet their needs and interests. GNVQs are flexible and enable students to keep their options open. Because Advanced level GNVQs are accepted as equivalent to A levels, students have the opportunity to go into higher education at a later date if they wish.

Further Reading

Applying for a Job, Judith Johnstone (How To Books).
Passing That Interview, Judith Johnstone (How To Books).
Writing a CV That Works, Paul McGee (How To Books).
These three books offer lots of really practical, down to earth help and advice on job-finding.

What Colour is Your Parachute: Richard Bolles (10 Speed Press).
An American classic – subtitled *A practical manual for job-hunters and career changers*, it is revised each year.

How to Master Selection Tests, Mike Bryon and Sanjay Modha (Kogan Page).
Explains what sorts of tests are used and gives lots of examples for practice.

Your Total Image, Philippa Davies (Judy Piatkus).
Examines different aspects of personal presentation and image projection.

Know Your Personality, Hans Eysenk and Glenn Wilson (Temple Smith).
The Book of Tests, Michael Nathenson (Fontana).
Both these titles offer lots of quizzes and tests to help you find out more about yourself.

How to Face Interviews, Clive Fletcher (Thorsons).
Succeed at Your Job Interview, George Heaviside (BBC Books).
Two practical and helpful books to help you prepare for the interview.

Assert Yourself, Gael Lindenfield (Thorsons).
Interesting and useful in developing asssertive behaviour.

On-line jobhunting

The Internet is expanding at a phenomenal rate. The information and URLs included here were accurate at the time this book went to press (summer 1999) but the situation can change very quickly. Search engines are easy to use and can keep you up to date with new sites.

ADVERTISEMENTS

http://www.appointments-plus.co.uk
Daily and *Sunday Telegraph* site. Specialises in engineering, sales manufacture and production. Includes on-line CV registration facility.

http://www.jobsunlimited.co.uk
Guardian and *Observer* jobs, volunteer opportunities and courses site. Set up to provide a 'personalised career manager', with a search engine pulling out and storing suitable vacancies.

AGENCIES

http://www.fres.co.uk
The Federation of Recruitment and Employment Service website gives guidelines on checking whether an agency is reputable.

http://www.cyberlink.co.uk/employ.html
A variety of links to useful sites for jobseekers.

http://www.gisajob.cgbin/body/cgi
Northamptonshire based recruitment website. Facility to submit on-line CV. Reckons to host around 20,000 jobs (mostly IT) from more than 600 agencies.

http://www.jobsearch.co.uk
Facility to submit on-line CV and search vacancies database.

http://www.topjobs.co.uk
Recruitment database searchable by region and job category.

http://www.digitext.co.uk
One of the many agencies offering IT vacancies.

http://www.reed.co.uk
A sophisticated site. Register with Reed Online and Job Sleuth will search out available vacancies in various job categories and locations. Mainly SE England.

Glossary

Aptitude tests. Tests intended to predict an individual's potential for particular types of work.

Assertiveness. Being assertive means communicating clearly and directly without being aggressive.

Commitment. An agreement of pledge (possibly unspoken) to do something.

CV – curriculum vitae. Latin for 'life timetable'. A CV is a summary of personal details, education, experience and skills.

Graphology. The study of an individual's handwriting to determine character.

Hierarchy. A body or organisation arranged according to rank.

Human resources. The skills, knowledge and experience of the workforce make up a company's human resources.

Induction. The process of initiation into the workplace. Induction for new employees may vary from an informal chat with a manager through to a formal course covering many aspects of the company.

Inter-personal skills. The general term 'inter-personal skills' is used to cover the technique of being good at getting on with people.

Jobclub. Jobclubs are part of the government's provision to help unemployed people find work. Jobclubs offer advice and guidance on job-hunting techniques and provide some free facilities (usually photocopying, postage and access to a phone). In return, Jobclub members usually agree to attend for specific sessions each week and to pursue job leads every day. More information from local Jobcentre.

Key skills. A general term embracing life skills which are important in the workspace. Key skills include communication, numeracy, information technology and personal skills including working with others.

Labour market. The term used to describe the supply and demand of people in the population who are working or seeking work.

Lateral thinking. Lateral means sideways. Lateral thinking means the ability to think creatively and make connections between disparate bits of information. It is associated with problem-solving.

Mentoring. A mentor is an experienced and trusted counsellor. Mentoring is a process where a new or inexperienced employee is assigned an experienced employee as their 'mentor' to help them learn their way around the workplace.

Motivate. To provide with an incentive or move to action. Motivation causes people to get things done. Motivation and self-motivation are prized qualities because they mean that someone has the internal drive and belief that goes with making decisions, acting on them and seeing things through.

Network. An inter-connected chain, group or system. Can exist physically, electronically or socially. For example, computer networks, telephone networks or the grapevine – a gossip network!

Numeracy. The ability to work with numbers and to use them to analyse and express facts, carry out basic calculations, handle figures, gather and process data.

Productivity. Producing or increasing worth or value of goods or services. Productivity may be an expression of output per employee.

Psychometric tests. Paper and pencils tests, devised by psychologists and intended to determine aptitudes, attainments and personality.

Recruitment agency/employment agency. Commercial recruitment or employment agencies operate in large towns and cities. Their business is to find staff to fill job vacancies notified by employers.

Referee/reference. In the context of job-hunting, a *referee* is someone who knows the job-hunter and will offer an opinion about character and abilities. They provide a *reference*, a statement of the qualifications and suitability of someone to do a particular job.

Service industry. Providing or distributing goods and services. Manufacturing industries make goods, while service industries supply and utilise them.

Telecommuting, teleworking. Telecommuting and teleworking are names given to the arrangement where workers spend some of their working week working at or from home. Contact with the office is maintained by plugging a home computer into the office computer via the telephone line.

Transferable skills. This term is used to describe capabilities which allow people to succeed in a wide range of different tasks and jobs.

Visualisation. Constructing a visual image or picture in the mind.

Vocational. Relating to work. Thus vocational courses are practical courses relating directly to jobs, and vocational skills are the ability to carry out work-related tasks.

VQs. National Vocational Qualifications, Scottish Vocational Qualifications and General National Vocational Qualification – NVQs/ SVQs/GNVQs – are work-related qualifications awarded to people for specific job skills.

Index

WRITING A CV THAT WORKS
Developing and using your key marketing tool

Paul McGee

What makes a CV stand out from the crowd? How can you present yourself in the most successful way? This practical book shows you how to develop different versions of your CV for every situation. Reveal your hidden skills, identify your achievements and learn how to communicate these successfully. Different styles and uses for a CV are examined, as you discover the true importance of your most powerful marketing tool. Paul McGee is a freelance Trainer and Consultant for one of Britain's largest outplacement organisations. He conducts marketing workshops for people from all walks of life.

128pp illus. 1 85703 365 5, 2nd edition.

LEARNING NEW JOB SKILLS
How and where to obtain the right training to help you get on at work

Laurel Alexander

This book presents a positive approach to education and training and will enable you to make considered and informed choices about improving your job prospects. Taking a training course will improve your confidence, prepare you for a job with a future, potentially increase your earnings and bring fresh challenge back into your lifre. There are guidelines on how to get funding for training courses, getting vocational training if you are unemployed and returning to study as a mature student. Laurel Alexander is a specialist trainer and writer in career development and has helped hundreds of adults improve their working lives.

128pp illus. 1 85703 375 2.

GETTING THAT JOB
The complete job finders handbook

Joan Fletcher

Now in its fourth edition this popular book provides a clear step-by-step guide to identifying job opportunities, writing successful application letters, preparing for interviews and being selected. 'A valuable book.' *Teachers Weekly*. 'Cheerful and appropriate . . . particularly helpful in providing checklists designed to bring system to searching for a job. This relaxed, friendly and very helpful little book could bring lasting benefit.' *Times Educational Supplement*. 'Clear and concise . . . should be mandatory reading by all trainees.' *Comlon Magazine* (LCCI). Joan Fletcher is an experienced Manager and Student Counsellor.

112pp illus. 1 85703 380 9. 4th edition.

STAYING AHEAD AT WORK
How to develop a winning portfolio of work skills and attitudes

Karen Mannering

The world of work is changing and employers are demanding more than just qualifications. To stay employed it is vital that you build a flexible portfolio of skills that say more about how you work and interact with others, than just the job you do. Getting ahead is tough, staying ahead can be tougher still. This book includes techniques to help you develop that 'something special' that will give you the edge over colleagues. You will also learn how to develop transportable soft skills that will ensure your future employability. Karen Mannering has worked extensively in the field of personal development, helping people build up a portfolio of skills that will enhance their professional careers.

128pp illus. 1 85703 298 5.

PASSING THAT INTERVIEW
Your step-by-step guide to coming out on top

Judith Johnstone

Using a systematic and practical approach, this book takes you step-by-step through the essential pre-interview groundwork, the interview encounter itself, and what you can learn from the experience. The book contains sample pre- and post-interview correspondence, and is complete with a guide to further reading, glossary of terms, and index. 'This is from the first class How To Books stable.' *Escape Committee Newsletter*. 'Offers a fresh approach to a well documented subject.' *Newscheck* (Careers Service Bulletin). 'A complete step-by-step guide.' *The Association of Business Executives*. Judith Johnstone is a Member of the Institute of Personnel & Development; she has been an instructor in Business Studies and adult literacy tutor, and has long experience of helping people at work.

144pp illus. 1 85703 538 0. 5th edition.

FINDING A JOB WITH A FUTURE
How to identify and work in growth industries and services

Laurel Alexander

If you want to ensure a long lasting career move in the right direction, you need to read this book which sets out in a practical way, growth areas of industry and commerce. Discover the work cycle of the future based on job specific skills, abstract skills, continuous learning and life-time career planning. Learn about flexible ways of working. Laurel Alexander is a manager/trainer in career development who has helped many individuals succeed in changing their work direction.

144pp illus. 1 85703 310 8.

WRITING BUSINESS LETTERS
How to produce day-to-day correspondence that is clear and effective

Ann Dobson

Intended for absolute beginners, this book uses fictional characters in a typical business setting to contrast the right and wrong ways to go about things. Taking nothing for granted, the book shows; how to plan a letter, how to write and present it, how to deal with requests, how to write and answer complaints, standard letters, personal letters, job applications, letters overseas, and a variety of routine and tricky letters. Good, bad and middling examples are used to help beginners see for themselves the right and wrong ways of doing things. Ann Dobson is Principal for a secretarial training school with long experience of helping people strengthen their business skills.

183pp illus. 1 85703 491 0. 3rd edition.

STARTING TO MANAGE
How to prepare yourself for a more responsible role at work

Julie-Ann Amos

This practical book gives a broad overview of management, to dispel much of the mystery which surrounds it. It is intended for all new managers, supervisors, students and anyone who hopes to enter management. It explains the various basic theories and puts these into a practical everyday context. The reader will learn how to manage: workloads, decisions, stock, equipment, money, legislation, customers, staff, and much more besides.

160pp illus. 1 85703 319 1.